FUN WITH WIRE

Books by Joseph Leeming

FUN WITH NATURECRAFT
FUN WITH GREETING CARDS
FUN WITH ARTIFICIAL FLOWERS
FUN WITH SHELLS
FUN WITH WIRE
FUN WITH PENCIL AND PAPER
FUN WITH BEADS
FUN FOR YOUNG COLLECTORS
HOLIDAY CRAFT AND FUN
FUN WITH FABRICS
FUN WITH CLAY
FUN WITH MAGIC
FUN WITH WOOD
FUN WITH LEATHER
FUN WITH PAPER
FUN WITH BOXES
THE COSTUME BOOK
FOR PARTIES AND PLAYS
FUN WITH PUZZLES
MORE FUN WITH MAGIC
PAPERCRAFT

FUN WITH WIRE

BY JOSEPH LEEMING

J. B. LIPPINCOTT COMPANY

PHILADELPHIA AND NEW YORK

The coat-hanger twists described and illustrated on pp. 70-71 are based on material appearing in *Popular Science Monthly*, copyright 1955 by Popular Science Publishing Co., Inc., and reproduced here by permission.

for
ETHEL KRUM MARMION
with thanks for her help

FOREWORD

Wire, like string, is one of the most common and most widely used materials. We see it every day, used in one way or another. But who knows what to do with it as a hobby? After talking with many people interested in handicrafts and hobbies, the answer seems to be: Very few people have as yet discovered the amount of fun you can have with wire.

After working with many other craft materials, I can say with genuine conviction that making things of wire is one of the most fascinating of all crafts. To most people —even veteran hobbyists—it should open up a whole new realm of possibilities.

Working with wire is a hobby that can give you endless hours of creative pleasure and satisfaction. This book is intended principally to open the reader's eyes to the possibilities, to describe the basic methods used in shaping and combining wire, and to give an idea of the almost limitless variety of things that can be made with it. It is my hope that it will start many people on a hobby that can bring them a great deal of pleasure and, if they are so minded, can bring them some financial profit as well.

Joseph Leeming

CONTENTS

CHAPTER ONE

WORKING WITH WIRE

Working with wire can be easy, simple and straightforward. It can also be tantalizing, tangled-up and frustrating. This is partly because people have a tendency to go ahead too fast and before they know it the wire is starting to kink and act up.

Their difficulties are also due to the fact that beginners, naturally enough, start to bend and work with wire with their fingers only. In many cases fingers are fine. But they definitely are not enough. Pliers and jigs—simple bending devices described below—are also needed, and it is these simple tools that will make you the master of the wire.

KINDS OF WIRE. There are many different kinds of wire, made of different materials—steel, iron, copper, brass, aluminum, silver and gold, among others. For most wirecraft articles, however, two of these are most commonly used. These are soft iron wire, sometimes called mild steel and sometimes wrought iron, and copper wire. Aluminum alloy wire is also excellent.

Soft iron wire is most frequently suggested for the articles described in this book. This does not mean, however, that it must always be used when it is suggested. The suggestion is meant to indicate that a pliable wire that will hold its shape should be used. Galvanized steel wire, copper wire, aluminum or coat-hanger wire can often be used instead.

Soft iron wire comes in all thicknesses, from very thin to thick rods ⅜ inch and more in diameter. The thinner kinds are sold on spools. The thicker wire rods are usually sold by hardware stores in 10-foot or 20-foot lengths. Most stores will, as a rule, saw off whatever length you want. Complete stocks of iron wire are available from craft and metal supply houses.

Galvanized steel wire is useful for many articles made of thin wire, and can often replace soft iron wire. Its silvery shine gives it an attractive appearance. It is a little stiffer than soft iron wire, but it is easy to bend and holds its shape well after bending.

Copper wire is made in thicknesses ranging from spider-web thin (.0100 of an inch) to ¼ inch. It is of two kinds. Plain copper wire is flexible and easy to handle, but fairly stiff. Annealed copper wire is soft and more flexible, yet retains its shape fairly well when bent. It is used for jewelry and can be used for other articles in which rigidity is not required.

Aluminum and aluminum alloy wires are excellent for all kinds of wire work in which absolute rigidity is not a necessity. You can get aluminum alloy wire at artist supply stores. It is quite inexpensive and comes in sizes ranging from ¹⁄₁₆ inch to ⅜ inch. It is ideal for many of the articles described in this book. I usually suggest soft iron wire in the text, partly because it is the traditional material. But aluminum alloy wire can usually be used and may be preferred by many readers. By all means find a store that sells this wire and get samples of it in different sizes. It is so easy to handle and bend that it makes the construction of almost any wire article a relatively simple matter.

Brass wire is stiffer than copper wire, but is not difficult to handle. It is useful for jewelry, and is excellent for achieving striking decorative effects, as in bird-cage planters or ornamental decorations for black wrought-iron lamp stands. Brass wire is not always carried in stock by hardware stores—even large stores. The best way to find the nearest source of supply, however, is to ask your local hardware dealer.

Gold and silver wire are used for jewelry and are fairly expensive. It is best, therefore, to use copper, brass or iron wire until you have gained experience. Even then, a customary practice is to make a piece of jewelry of copper wire first, to be sure you can do a good job, and make only the final article of the more expensive gold or silver wire.

Coat-hanger wire can be used for many of the articles described in this book, even though its use may not always be specified. This wire is about $\frac{1}{16}$ inch thick and is tough and springy. Consequently, it should be handled with pliers and jigs to make accurate and clean-cut bends.

There is a simple way, however, to soften coat-hanger wire and make it easier to handle. Put the coat hangers in a small wood fire. The heat will soften the wire. Clean the wire with steel wool after it has cooled. You may often wish to get rid of the shiny finish before painting it a dull satin black or some other color. The finish can be removed with steel wool or sandpaper.

WIRE GAUGES. The thickness of wire is denoted by its gauge, such as 8-gauge wire, 14-gauge wire, and so on. The lower the gauge, the thicker the wire. The higher the gauge, the thinner the wire. Thus, 8-gauge wire is much thicker than 18-gauge wire.

Two gauges are in common use in the United States. The Steel Wire Gauge is used for wire made of iron and steel. The Brown & Sharpe (B & S) gauge, also called the American Wire Gauge, is used for copper wire and wire of all metals and alloys other than iron and steel. These gauges, for the sizes of wire most commonly used, are given below.

STEEL WIRE GAUGE

Gauge	Thickness in inches	Gauge	Thickness in inches
1	.2830	11	.1205 *(about ⅛″)*
2	.2625	12	.1055
3	.2437 *(about ¼″)*	13	.0915
4	.2253	14	.0800
5	.2070	15	.0720
6	.1920 *(about ³⁄₁₆″)*	16	.0625 *(about ¹⁄₁₆″)*
7	.1770	17	.0540
8	.1620	18	.0475
9	.1483	19	.0410
10	.1350	20	.0348

BROWN & SHARPE (B & S) GAUGE
For copper, aluminum and nonferrous alloy wires

Gauge	Thickness in inches	Gauge	Thickness in inches
1	.2893	11	.0907
2	.2576 *(about ¼″)*	12	.0808
3	.2294	13	.0720
4	.2043	14	.0641 *(about ¹⁄₁₆″)*
5	.1819 *(about ³⁄₁₆″)*	15	.0571
6	.1620	16	.0508
7	.1443	17	.0453
8	.1285 *(about ⅛″)*	18	.0403
9	.1144	19	.0359
10	.1019	20	.0320

Since most people are not familiar with the wire gauges and find it confusing (at least at first) to be told to use, say, 14-gauge wire, I have avoided mentioning gauges in the text. Instead, the thickness of the wire is given in fractions of an inch. This course is followed, also, because the two gauges differ from each other. Consequently, 14-gauge copper, brass or aluminum wire (about

⅟₁₆ inch thick) is not the same thickness as 14-gauge steel or iron wire, which is about ⅟₁₂ inch thick.

The section on wire jewelry is an exception. There I specify the gauge, because jewelry is made for the most part from copper, brass, silver and gold wire, all of which are measured by the same gauge. Also, the making of wire jewelry has become quite a widespread hobby and it has become customary in this field to designate the wire by gauge.

HANDLING THIN WIRE. Thin wire is usually sold on spools. When unwinding, always draw the wire straight away from the side of the spool, as in Fig. 1. This will keep it straight and free from kinks.

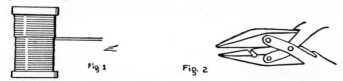

Fig 1   Fig. 2

Be careful not to bend thin wire back and forth too often in the same place. This makes the wire brittle and causes it to break.

Pay attention to the natural curve of the wire. All thin wire has such a curve, and it is easier to work with it than against it. Accordingly, when you are making a curving design, bend the wire in the direction of its natural curve, which is the way the wire wants to go. This applies particularly to the making of wire jewelry.

CUTTING AND FILING WIRE. Thin wire is cut with wire nippers, with tin shears, or with wire-cutting pliers. There is no difficulty about this. Thicker wire rod is cut with a hacksaw.

After wire is cut its ends are sharp and should usually be filed smooth. Use a small half-round file and use forward strokes only. Do not rub the file back and forth. The filing will keep the wire from scratching or cutting your hands.

Bending Thin Wire. Thin wire is bent with smooth-jawed, flat-nose pliers, or with a small pair of parallel chain pliers like those shown in Fig. 2. Bending jigs are also needed, however, to make neat and uniform bends, loops and twists.

Fig. 3 shows two jigs for making spiral coils or springs. One is simply a pencil, a knitting needle, a nail or some other fairly small round article. When making a coil, be sure to wind the wire straight up and down, as shown, and keep the coils of wire as close to each other as possible.

Jigs of this kind are sometimes called *mandrels*, a word which designates any object that is used as a core around which wire is bent to make a spiral coil or spring. They may be round, oval, square, rectangular, triangular, or any other shape.

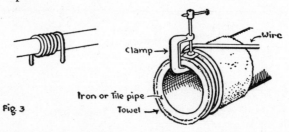

Fig. 3

The other jig in Fig. 3 is for heavier wire and consists of a piece of iron or tile pipe with a towel or piece of card-board wrapped around it to prevent scratching the wire. A clamp is used to hold the wire in place while you make the coils.

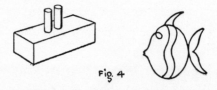

Fig. 4

Fig. 4 shows a simple but extremely useful jig. It can be used for many types of simple bending such as, for example, the fish wall decoration shown. It can handle coat-hanger wire or ⅛-inch soft iron wire. The jig consists of two pegs of ⅜-inch dowel or two large nails, set in a wooden base. The nails should be wrapped with cloth to prevent marking the wire.

For coat-hanger wire or ⅛-inch iron wire, the pegs should be ³⁄₁₆ inch apart. When bending wire with this jig, place it between the pegs and feed it through slowly, bending it a very little at a time to avoid making kinks or flat spots. Check the bending frequently with a full-sized drawing of the piece you are making. After finishing the bending, check to see that each wire part lies flat and has no twist.

Fig. 5

Fig. 5 shows a jig for making wire hoops or arches. The main part is a circular piece of wood of the required size, fastened to the wooden base with a screw or nail.

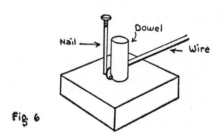

Fig 6

Fig. 6 shows a jig that is useful for making many simple curved bends. It is a short piece of dowel of the size required and a nail driven into a wooden base.

The jig in Fig. 7 is for making loops of the kind shown, which are used in wire jewelry. It consists of six small nails driven into a wooden base. The nails are spaced so as to make the loops of the desired size.

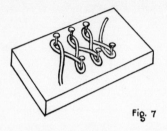

Fig. 7

BENDING HEAVY WIRE. Heavy wire, from ⅛ inch to ⅜ inch thick, can be bent without heating. A vise and a hammer, together with various kinds of jigs, are the principal tools employed. Most of the basic bends are shown in Fig. 8.

Angle bends are made as shown at A, by clamping the wire in a vise and pounding it with a hammer. Do the bending a little at a time. When nearing completion, check the angle against a template cut to the required angle from cardboard or hardboard. A right-angle or 90-degree bend can be checked with a try square.

You can also bend wire by hand, provided the wire is not too thick. When you do this, slip a short length of pipe over the end of the wire to increase the leverage.

A very useful bending tool is a bar or block of metal with a hole bored through it, as shown at B. You can get such a device at some large hardware stores or, more likely, at a builder's supply store, by asking for a hex bar.

Rings or circles are formed by bending the wire around a metal rod of the required size, as shown at C. Eyes are formed by the same method, as at D. The eye is formed by first making a ring and then bending back the rest of the wire by hand or with a hammer. Square bends are made with the aid of a hardwood block, as at E. Gradual bends of all kinds can be hammered on any type of round anvil or metal bar, as at F.

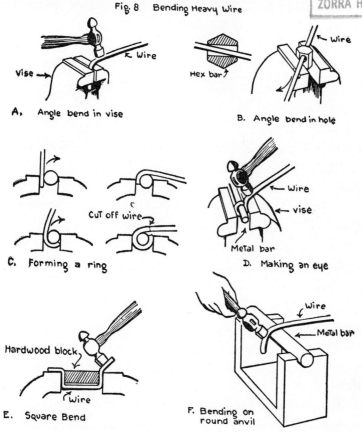

Fig. 8 Bending Heavy Wire

A. Angle bend in vise

Hex bar

Wire

B. Angle bend in hole

Cut off wire

C. Forming a ring

Wire

vise

Metal bar

D. Making an eye

Hardwood block

Wire

E. Square Bend

Wire

Metal bar

F. Bending on round anvil

A homemade bending jig of the kind shown in Fig. 9 can be used for making all kinds of gradual curves or scrolls. The jig consists of two wooden forms screwed to a wood base. When using such a jig, form the curves gradually with a series of gradual bends.

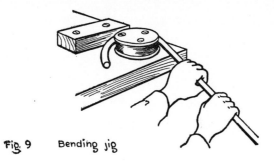

Fig. 9   Bending jig

A jig for making wire legs for small tables and stands is shown in Fig. 10. It illustrates how you can make jigs to form almost any kind of shape you wish to make. The jig shown can be made by setting pieces of pipe or dowel in holes drilled in a wooden base. Round blocks of wood screwed or nailed to a base could also be used.

JOINING AND FASTENING WIRE. Welding is the time-honored method of joining together wire and wire rod used in making articles of wrought iron or soft iron. But welding is a special art, requiring fairly expensive equipment, and it is not really needed. There are other ways of fastening that will provide a secure joint.

Solder can be used, and you can try it out if you wish. Today you can get inexpensive soldering kits at the ten-cent stores, which require only oven heat. These kits are easy to use and are worth experimenting with. There are also new liquid or plastic solders which require no heat.

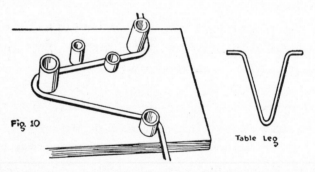

Fig. 10   Table Leg

The best all-around way of joining wires together is probably by the use of one of the new cements or adhesives. These are much stronger than glue, and can bind metal to metal very securely. Some of these cements are of the metallic cold-solder type. They are sold under a dozen or more trade names and are composed of iron, steel or aluminum powder mixed with a plastic bonding agent. They come in liquid form and also in the form of a paste.

They harden into a rigid, steel-like mass which can be filed, sanded, buffed and even machined.

Other kinds of adhesives, such as the so-called iron cements and miracle adhesives also make strong bonds. When using these cements, the parts being joined should be held together with clamps, if possible, while the cement hardens.

When making articles which must bear some strain, it is always best to use both cement and twisted wire. Cement the parts together first. Then wind wire around them and coat the wire with cement. In the text I do not always specify the use of both cement and twisted wire. As a rule, I say simply: "Cement the wires together," rather than repeating over and over: "Use twisted wire also if the join seems to require the extra strength." Therefore, take it as said here once and for all: Make the joins as strong as they need to be, using one or more of the methods suggested here.

When cementing together the two ends of a wire circle, always push the ends past each other so they overlap. Then draw them back in line and cement them. In some cases, you can join the ends of a circle made of thin wire by overlapping the ends and then securing the overlap with cement or cement and twisted wire.

In making shelves or shadow boxes or the kinds of hanging flower-pot holders that must bear a weight, cement and twisted wire should be reinforced with stiff wire or metal supports or brackets. Fig. 11 shows how these are most commonly used.

Another way of making a strong join at a corner is to use an L-shaped bracket made of scrap sheet metal. Coat the inside of the bracket with cement.

Fig. 11 also shows how metal or plastic tubing, or even thin sheet metal, can be used to join the two ends of a wire

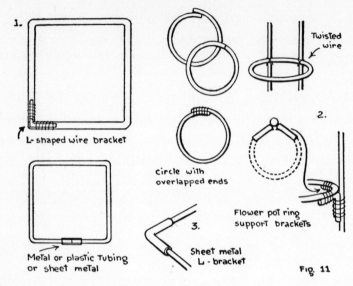

1.

L-shaped wire bracket

Metal or plastic tubing
or sheet metal

circle with
overlapped ends

Twisted
wire

2.

3.

Sheet metal
L-bracket

Flower pot ring
support brackets

Fig. 11

frame. In this case, the join is made in the center of one part of the frame, instead of at a corner. The smallest metal tubing is ⅛ inch. Accordingly, with thinner wire, sheet metal should be coated with cement and wrapped around the ends that are to be joined. For joins of this type on small objects where there is no strain, cellulose or other tape can be used.

PLANNING AND MEASURING. When making many of the articles described in this book, it is best to make a full-scale drawing to use as a guide. This drawing will give you all, or many, of the exact measurements you will need, and will also serve as a guide in bending the wire correctly. I have not repeated this over and over, but please take it as specific advice—and very good and necessary advice.

In some cases I have suggested specific measurements. But in most cases I have left the measurements up to the reader. This is because the approximate measurements are in most cases obvious, and also because many of the pieces can be made in a number of different sizes, the size depending on the place which the article is going to occupy. For the same reason, I do not always specify the gauge or thickness of wire to use, though I have tried to indicate as often as possible the approximate thickness that is commonly used.

A full-sized drawing will give you the lengths of wire needed for many pieces. There are other articles, however, which are made in such a way that a two-dimensional drawing will not indicate the lengths of all the parts. In such cases, it is best to make a model, using easily-bent wire solder or thin soft iron wire. You can then remove the different wires that make up the model and measure them to determine the exact length needed for the stiffer wires of the finished product.

PAINTING. The most commonly used finish for most articles made of soft iron is flat, dull or satin-black paint. This gives a black wrought-iron effect. The paint can be applied with a brush or, if it is well thinned, with a fly sprayer.

Any colors other than black can, of course, be used; and with many articles a brighter color is suitable or preferable.

CHAPTER TWO

WIRECRAFT HOUSEHOLD ARTICLES

PACK HORSE PENHOLDER. The saddle holds pens and pencils; the clip that forms the horse's head holds letters, memos, bills or even recipes; and rings or keys can be hung on the tail.

The neck and body of the horse are made of two pieces of $\frac{1}{16}$-inch soft iron wire shaped as shown in the drawing. The left-hand ends of the wires are cemented into two holes drilled in a wooden clip. Once the body is made, all that remains is to cement in place the four pieces that form the legs and the saddle. These may be of $\frac{1}{16}$-inch or slightly thinner wire.

PENCIL HOLDER. Use $\frac{1}{16}$-inch soft iron wire or coat-hanger wire for the four legs and the circle to which they are cemented. Each leg is bent over at the top so

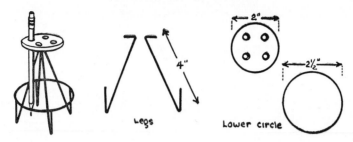

that it can be cemented to the circle of wood or plastic that forms the top. Make the holder about 4 inches high.

The wire circle is about 2½ inches in diameter and the wood or plastic circle 2 inches in diameter. Drill four $\frac{5}{16}$-inch holes in the top to hold the pencils. If you do not have tools with which to shape and drill wood or plastic, you can use a piece of thick cardboard for the circular top piece.

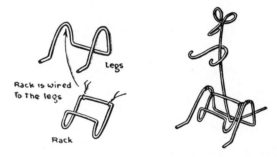

KANGAROO MEMO PAPER HOLDER. This animal can be put together quite easily, using $\frac{1}{16}$-inch or heavier iron or copper wire for his body and hind legs and thinner wire for his forelegs. The head can be made of twisted wire or papier-mâché, or it can be a cork or a whittled piece of wood.

The kangaroo has three main pieces. One is his body and tail. The second is his hind legs. The part of the wire that stretches across the back of this piece passes beneath the tail and is cemented to the tail. The rack for memo paper is then fastened to the legs with twisted wire and cement added to strengthen the join.

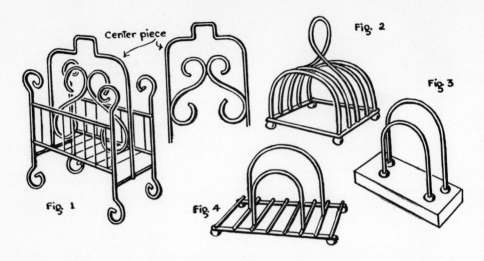

STATIONERY AND PAPER HOLDERS. Use 1/16-inch or heavier wire, brass or aluminum wire for the holders that have wire hoops. If iron wire is used, it can be painted black or some bright color. A piece of wood or plastic makes the base of the holder shown in Fig. 3, while wires form the bases of the others. The wood or plastic base should be about 6 inches long and 3 inches wide. Drill holes to take the ends of the wire hoops and cement the ends firmly in place.

The construction of the three all-wire holders is made clear in the drawings. The ends of the wire crosspieces in the two-hoop holder (Fig. 4) are painted black, red or some other color. Beads or balls are cemented beneath the four corners.

HARDWARE CLOTH LETTER RACK. Hardware cloth is a wire-mesh screening that is inexpensive and easy to work with. It is a handy material, useful in making wire articles of various kinds in addition to the letter rack illustrated here. The rack is made from a piece of hardware cloth measuring about 7 by 14 inches, which is bent to the shape shown. Bend over the outside edge, top and sides, and bend that under to make a smooth finish. If you wish, you can bind the edges all around with raffia or colored string. When the rack is completed, paint it black or some other color.

SPIRAL-COIL LETTER RACK. These wire coil racks will help to keep a desk tidy by keeping letters, bills and other papers in order. They make good paper-napkin holders, too.

Use ⅟₁₆-inch or heavier soft iron wire or copper wire, and make the coils on a round mandrel such as a tin can or a piece of pipe. The 16 coils should be about 2½ inches in diameter. When the coils have been completed, bunch them tightly together at the bottom and spread out the tops. Bend down the left-hand coil so it will lie flat on a table, and cement its free end to the bottom of several of the other coils. At the right-hand end bend the last coil down flat and then use the free end of the wire to form the neck and head of the "animal" which the rack more or less represents. With light-weight wire, the coils can be held together at the bottom by a piece of wire twisted around them.

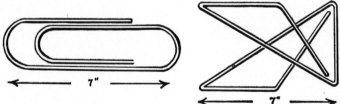

GIANT PAPER CLIPS. These giant paper clips can be used to hold together batches of papers and letters. Use ⅟₁₆-inch or slightly heavier copper, brass or soft iron wire. The oval clip is about 7 inches long and 1¾ inches wide, outside dimensions. The other clip should also be about 7 inches long. Use jigs made of dowel or other round material to make smooth curves, and use a wooden mallet to hammer the clips flat after you have finished the bending.

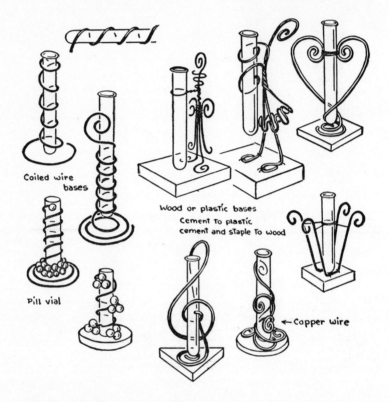

Coiled wire bases

Pill vial

Wood or plastic bases
Cement to plastic
cement and staple to wood

←Copper wire

BUD-VASE HOLDERS. The drawings show several different kinds of wire bud-vase holders, designed to hold test tubes or pill vials containing flowers. All the holders are easy to make and the drawings show just how the wire is bent or curved for each one.

The heart-shaped, V-shaped and treble-clef-shaped holders are fastened to wooden bases with staples. Any kind of wire may be used—copper, galvanized steel, soft iron, brass or coat-hanger wire. The wooden base pieces are painted to harmonize with the wire used in the supports.

LEAF HOOKS. These wire leaves not only decorate your walls but also provide handy hooks for anything from pot holders to garments. Make them of 1/16-inch or thinner soft iron wire and paint them black or some other color. Each leaf should be about 7 inches high. The hooks are made of 1/8-inch wire and are fastened in place with wire twisted around the backbone of the leaf.

The outlines can be enhanced by the use of double wires at some places. The extra wires should be thinner than those used for the main outlines, and coiled or twisted around the basic wire.

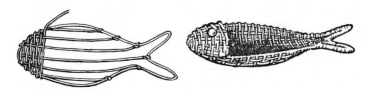

FISH-SHAPED BASKET. This is a reproduction of a basket that has been made for centuries by Spanish peasants. It can be any size you wish, depending on whether it is to be used for candies and nuts or for fruits.

Make the frame from 1/16-inch iron or other wire, cementing the ends together. Then set in the ribs, which may be of lighter wire. Twist the ends of the ribs around the frame. Then weave thinner wire across from side to side, passing over and under the ribs. Add the head when the rest of the fish has been completed. Cement a button or bead to the head to make the eye.

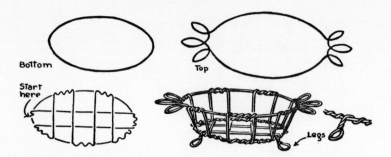

TWIST-WIRE BASKET. This wire basket, when lined with a napkin, can be used for candies or nuts. It can be made of copper, steel, iron or other wire. The bottom is made of two pieces. One is a wire circle or oval with ends twisted or cemented together. The other is a wire that is twisted to the oval as shown. The top consists of a larger circle or oval with loops at two sides. The top and bottom are joined by a single piece of fairly stiff wire twisted to both pieces as shown. Legs may be added.

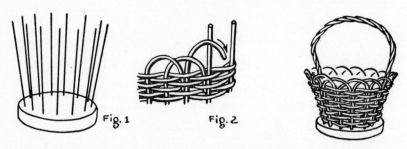

CORK-BASE BASKETS. Flat corks make good bases for wire baskets. You can get them in different sizes at a ten-cent store.

The ribs of a basket may be straight pieces of wire or else wire hoops. In either case they are pushed into the cork base, which will hold them firmly. Use fine wire for the basket's sides. Twist one end around one of the uprights and then wind it around, weaving it over and under the alternate uprights. Secure the wire at the top with a twist, and add a handle if you wish.

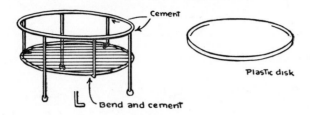

WIRE AND PLASTIC CENTERPIECE. This simply designed centerpiece makes an attractive setting for fruit, vegetable or Christmas-ball arrangements. It is good-looking in brass and also in iron wire painted black.

The bottom is most easily made from a circular cake-cooling rack. The circular top rail of ⅟₁₆-inch or heavier wire can be bent to shape around the bottom, for this will make it just the right size. Cement the ends of the top rail together, in preference to twisting. The three legs are cemented to the top rail and to the bottom piece. The three side supports are cemented to the top rail and are bent inwards at the bottom. A circular piece of white or colored plastic is cut to fit over the bottom. A diameter of about 8 inches is a good size for this piece.

CANDY-DISH HOLDER. This can be made of ⅟₁₆-inch or slightly thinner wire. Copper wire is left unpainted, while iron or steel wire may be painted black or some other color. Adapt the depth and diameter of the holder to a specific dish. The construction is simple and is made clear in the drawings. Round the ends of the legs with a file or cement them into beads, buttons or rubber tips.

Wire base   Hardboard base

SIMPLE FRUIT HOLDER. The base of this fruit holder can be made of wire or of Masonite or other hardboard. The side arches are made of $\frac{1}{16}$-inch or thinner iron, brass or other wire. Their ends are bent to form hooks which are hooked over the rim of a wire base or are stapled to a hardboard base. Use a large tin can or some other round jig in order to make all the arches exactly the same. The holder may have a 6-inch-diameter base or be slightly larger.

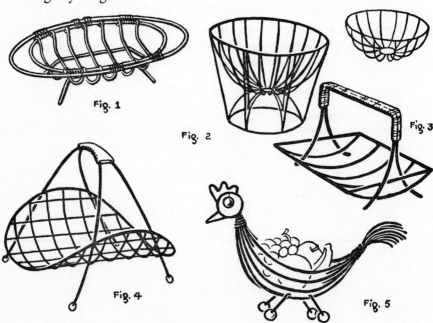

Fig. 1

Fig. 2

Fig. 3

Fig. 4

Fig. 5

FRUIT CONTAINERS. It is fun to make many kinds of wire containers for fruit. All the different kinds may be used, depending on your own preference. Soft iron wire painted black is one of the most popular types for these containers.

The drawings show the construction of the container in Fig. 1. It consists of a large oval, which forms the top and the handles, and a smaller oval fastened to it with cement and, for certain strength, with twisted wire. The ends of the ribs are bent to form hooks. These are hooked over the rim of the smaller oval and the hooks are pinched tight with pliers.

A good way to make the bowl which forms the top of the container in Fig. 2 is to cement the curved ribs to a circular metal key ring or to a small circle of wire, placed at the center of the bottom of the bowl. Bend each rib on the same jig and check them against each other to make sure that they are all identical in curvature.

Fig. 3 is easy to make and its construction is shown in the drawing. Its handle can be wound with raffia, which makes a good contrast with black-painted wire.

The container shown in Fig. 4 will take a little time and patience to make. Its construction is simple, however, and presents no special difficulties. It is a good idea to wrap raffia around the top of the handles, both for good looks and to add extra strength to the join. The handles themselves should be fastened at that point with both cement and twisted wire.

The main part of the rooster container shown in Fig. 5 is made from nine pieces of $\frac{1}{16}$-inch soft iron wire curved to shape. Draw the wire through a simple bending jig consisting of two dowels or nails on a piece of board, as illustrated in CHAPTER ONE. The wires that form the body of the container also form the tail feathers.

Fasten the body wires together at the head end with cement and twisted wire. Wrap thin wire around the body wires at the point where they turn into the tail feathers and coat the wrapping with cement. The circular head is fastened to the body with twisted wire, and the beak and comb are cemented to the head.

For the legs, bend two wires to make pairs of legs, shaping the crosspiece to fit the curved base of the body, and cement in place and bind with fine wire.

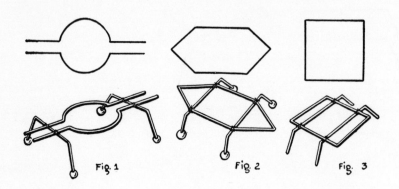

MODERN TRIVETS. The trivets are made with 1/16-inch to 1/8-inch iron wire painted black. Use a round jig, such as a tin can or a piece of pipe, to make the semicircles in Fig. 1 identical, and use a full-scale drawing to check the angles of the trivet shown in Fig. 2. The legs are cemented to the top pieces and the join can be reinforced with twisted wire coated with cement if you consider it necessary. File the ends of the legs round or insert them in small wooden or plastic balls.

TILE-HOLDER TRIVETS. You can put any tile into these black-painted wire holders and by doing so convert the tile into a handsome trivet. The holders are usually made for a 6-inch-square tile and are fine for flower stands or for table use.

Each holder consists of a square of 1/16-inch or heavier soft iron wire designed to surround a tile, which rests on a base made of wires bent to shape and cemented together. The drawings show several designs, which differ from each other chiefly in the shapes of the handles or the method of ornamentation.

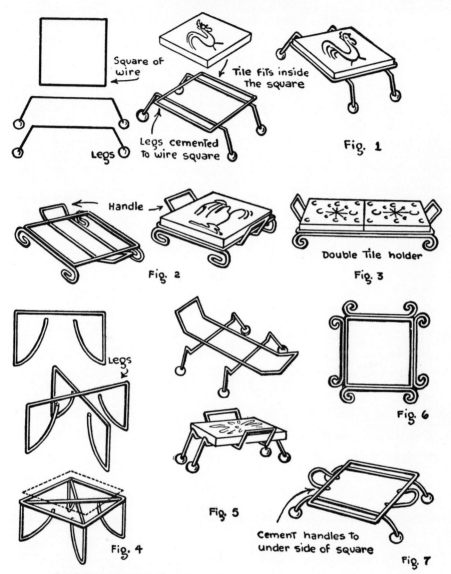

Square of wire

Tile fits inside the square

Legs cemented to wire square

Legs

Fig. 1

Handle

Double Tile holder

Fig. 2

Fig. 3

Legs

Fig. 6

Fig. 5

Cement handles to under side of square

Fig. 4

Fig. 7

CANDLE HOLDERS. Here are six interesting wire candle holders.

The holder in Fig. 1 consists of three pieces of ⅛-inch or heavier soft iron wire bent to identical curves and cemented together. Short upright pieces of ⅛-inch or ³⁄₁₆-inch wire, 1 inch long, are cemented to them. Candle brackets are cemented to the tops of the short pieces.

You can buy candle brackets at hardware, department and ten-cent stores, or you can make your own. They can be made of two pieces of sheet metal cemented together, or of plastic or metal tubing cemented to a plastic or sheet metal base. A large iron nut from a hardware store cemented to a sheet metal or plastic base makes a good bracket with a wrought-iron effect. The threads inside the nuts help to hold candles snug.

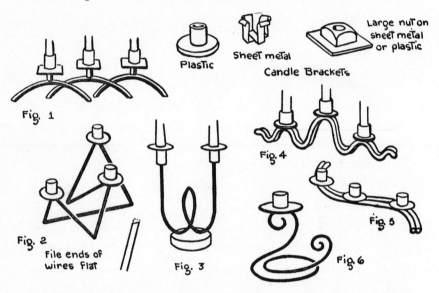

Plastic

Sheet metal

Large nut on sheet metal or plastic

Candle Brackets

Fig. 1

Fig. 2

File ends of wires flat

Fig. 3

Fig. 4

Fig. 5

Fig. 6

The holder in Fig. 2 is made of three pieces of $\frac{1}{16}$-inch or heavier iron wire, which hold three candles at different levels. Make one of the pieces first. Then use it as a guide for the size of the other two. It is a good idea when making the last two pieces to model them first in wire solder or thin soft iron wire. The models will help in making the bends correctly in the heavier wire. Since the wire supports slant, it is necessary to bevel their top ends with a file to make a flat support for the candle brackets.

Fig. 3 consists simply of a single piece of $\frac{1}{8}$-inch wire bent to the shape shown and cemented to a wood base.

Figs. 4 and 5 are made of two $\frac{3}{16}$-inch or $\frac{1}{4}$-inch iron wires cemented together to form a wide enough support for the candle brackets. The holder in Fig. 6 is made from a single piece of ⅛-inch wire bent to the shape shown. The handle should be cemented or fastened with twisted wire to the circular base.

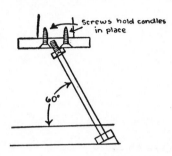

Screws hold candles in place

60°

WIRE AND WOOD CANDLE HOLDER. The base of this candle holder is a circular piece of ¾-inch-thick wood with a 5-inch diameter. The candles are mounted on small wooden disks made of ¼-inch-thick wood, each having a diameter of 1½ inches.

With a pair of compasses make a 3-inch circle in the center of the base. At three equidistant points along its circumference drill three ¼-inch holes at angles of 60 degrees. To make all the holes at the same angle first drill a guide hole at the correct angle in a separate block of wood. Then use this piece as a jig by clamping it to the base and drilling through the guide hole to make each of the holes in the base.

Drill 60-degree holes in the three small disks and insert two screws in each disk, as shown, to hold the candles. Then cement three 6-inch-long pieces of ¼-inch soft iron wire into the holes in the small disks and base.

CANDLE SCONCES. The designs of these sconces are simple but very effective. The bends are all easy to make with the aid of simple jigs. Use ¹⁄₁₆-inch or heavier soft iron wire and fasten the pieces together with cement and twisted wire where needed.

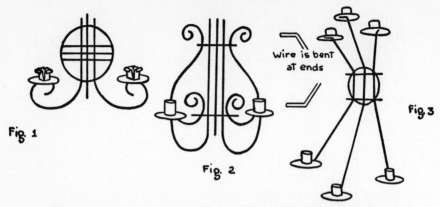

You can buy ready-made candle brackets at some hardware and ten-cent stores, but it is not difficult to make
your own. Use plastic or metal tubing or else large iron
nuts, and cement them to circular bases of plastic or thin
sheet metal.

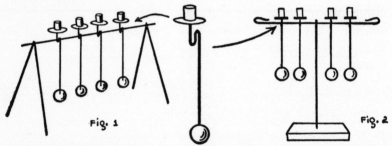

CANDLE SWINGS. Candle swings are a special kind
of candle holder that originated in Sweden. The wire
supports are hooked over a rod and are weighted with
colored wooden balls. This permits the candles to swing
slightly and throw moving lights about the room.

The drawings show two kinds of supports for the
swinging candles. Both are made of ⅛-inch soft iron wire.
The pieces are cemented together and the fastenings are
reinforced with twisted wire. The wires that support the
candles are ¹⁄₁₆-inch or thinner soft iron wire. The candle
brackets can be made of plastic or metal tubing cemented
to plastic or sheet-metal bases. Large iron nuts cemented
to plastic or sheet-metal bases may also be used.

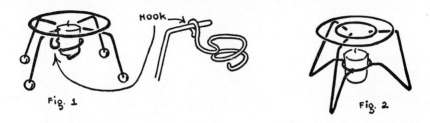

CANDLE WARMERS. Two kinds of candle warmers are shown in the drawings, both made of ⅟₁₆-inch to ⅛-inch iron wire. The parts are all easy to make, with the possible exception of the legs of the holder in Fig. 2. Make a full-sized drawing of one leg and use it as a guide to help in making all three legs identical. The spiral candle holder used in the holder in Fig. 1 is hooked over the top bar of one of the legs and the hook is then pinched tight with pliers.

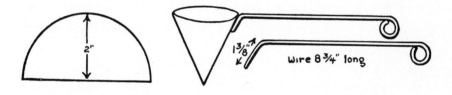

CANDLE SNUFFER. Use 6-gauge (a little less than ³⁄₁₆-inch) copper wire for the handle, and make it about 9 inches long. Bend a loop in one end, using a jig of the kind illustrated in CHAPTER ONE. Then hammer the other end flat and bend it as shown.

The bowl is made of .016-inch soft brass. It is formed into a cone with your fingers and long-nosed pliers, and the seam is closed by tapping it with a light hammer. Flutes can be made in the rim with pliers, if desired. The handle is fastened to the bowl with one of the cements that will withstand heat. When completed, the snuffer is polished and given a coat of clear lacquer.

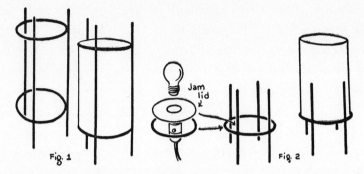

HURRICANE LAMPS. The simple and modern-looking lamps shown in the drawings are attractive and easy to make. Either ⅟₁₆-inch or ⅛-inch wire can be used.

The lamp in Fig. 1 consists of two wire circles about 4 inches in diameter, to which three legs are cemented. The shade may be of parchment paper or Fiberglas. It is cemented to the framework. A metal jar cap, with a hole cut in its center large enough to fit the lamp socket you plan to use, is cemented to the lower circle. Line the small circle with electrical rubber tape for insulation and to make the socket fit tightly.

The lamp in Fig. 2 has four short legs which are cemented to a wire ring. It is intended to hold a translucent glass shade, but parchment paper can also be used.

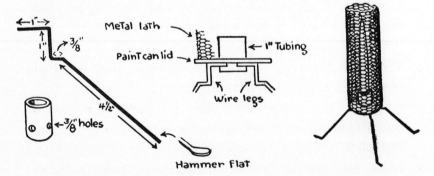

WIRE-MESH HURRICANE LAMP. For these Candle lamps with wire-mesh screen chimneys use ³⁄₁₆-inch soft iron wire rod for the three legs. Bend the legs together to make them identical, and hammer the ends flat to serve as feet. Then cut a 1¼-inch length of 1-inch diameter plastic or metal tubing to serve as the candle holder. Drill three ³⁄₁₆-inch holes near its bottom end, spacing them 120 degrees apart. These are for the legs. With a file, bevel the inside of the top to permit easy insertion of the candle.

Make the circular base from a 3-inch-diameter paint-can lid. Cut a 1-inch hole in its center. Insert the legs in the holes in the tubing, slip the can lid over the tubing upside down, and cement or solder the legs to both the lid and the tubing.

The screen chimney is made of expanded-metal lath, which you can get at a hardware store. Cut a piece measuring 9 inches by 9½ inches, with the 9½-inch dimension along the wavy finished edge of the lath, which is to be at the top of the chimney. Roll this piece around a pipe or a rolling pin to make a cylinder that will fit tightly over the flange of the can lid. Fasten the two ends of the cylinder by cementing or soldering, using twisted wires, or by hooking parts of one end around the other.

LAMP BASES. Wire can be used to make many different kinds of lamps. Black-painted wire achieves a wrought-iron effect, but brass wire is often used in combination with the black to make a vivid contrast.

Of the lamps shown in the drawings, in all cases the wires are fastened at the top to a wire circle or a block of wood with a circular hole drilled through its center. With a wire ring, the support wires can be cemented directly to the sides of the ring, or they can be hooked over the ring and pinched tightly in place with pliers. If you use a wood block, the support wires are cemented into holes drilled at an angle in the under side of the block.

The wire circle or the hole in the wood block should be large enough to hold the electric light socket you plan to

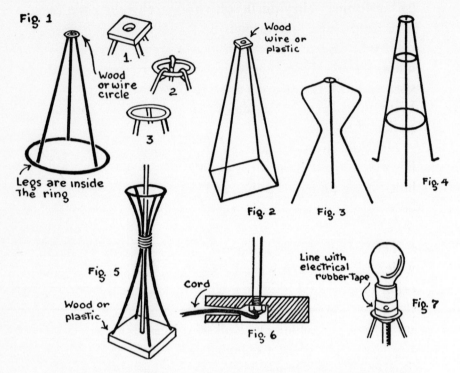

Fig. 1

1.

Wood or wire circle

2

3

Legs are inside the ring

Wood wire or plastic

Fig. 2　Fig. 3

Fig. 4

Fig. 5

Wood or plastic

Cord

Line with electrical rubber Tape

Fig. 6

Fig. 7

use. It is a good idea to line the circle or hole with electrical rubber tape for insulation and to make the socket fit tightly. If a wire circle is too large for the socket, you can cement on top of it a metal circle cut from a jar cap with a hole of the right size cut in its center.

Standard lamp fittings can be purchased from a hardware store or salvaged from old lamps.

The electric cord leading to the lamp can be passed through a vertical piece of threaded metal pipe ⅜ inch in diameter, which you can buy in any length you want. If this is done, use a wooden base, instead of a wire circle or square, cement the pipe into a hole drilled in the base, and fasten it with a nut. Then drill a hole in one side of the block for the cord to pass through and reach the bottom of the pipe (Fig. 6). The lamp socket is then screwed on to the top of the pipe.

Coat-hanger wire can be used for the lighter parts of these lamp bases, and ⅛-inch or ³⁄₁₆-inch soft iron wire rod for the supports. The support wires in the lamp shown in Fig. 5 are held together with a wire circle, with twisted wire, or with a ready-made metal or plastic ring.

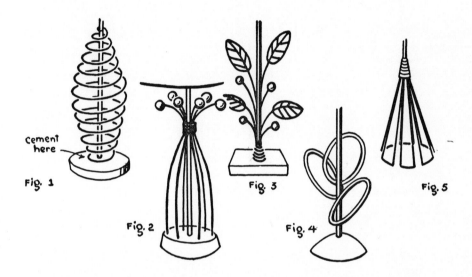

Cement here

Fig. 1

Fig. 2

Fig. 3

Fig. 4

Fig. 5

LAMP-BASE DECORATIONS. Instead of making an entire lamp, you can have an interesting time adding decorative wire designs to the bases of old lamps. The decorations can usually be made of ¹⁄₁₆-inch to ⅛-inch wire, and the kind of wire to be used is determined by the character of the lamp. Iron wire painted black goes with wrought iron, brass wire with brass, and so on. Brass wire decorations combined with wrought-iron standards are very popular, and they give a stunning effect.

In all the examples shown in the drawings the wire pieces are cut, bent to shape and cemented in place. Wire solder or thin soft iron wire can be used to make preliminary models to get the correct measurements of the different pieces. Where there are a number of wires bent to the same shape, a jig should be used to ensure uniformity.

FLOWER POT HOLDERS. The drawings show a number of single pot holders; two- and three-pot holders can readily be devised as variations of similar construction. They can be made in different sizes and of different thicknesses of wire to hold pots of varying dimensions. Usually, ³⁄₁₆-inch soft iron wire is the most suitable.

Most of the holders are made by cementing together pieces of wire which are either straight or bent to different shapes. The wires of the basket type of holder can be fastened to the bottom and top rings either by twisting or cementing. You can make the chair holder either a rocking chair or a straight-legged chair. It is painted red, yellow or some other bright color, and is intended to hold only a small-sized flower pot.

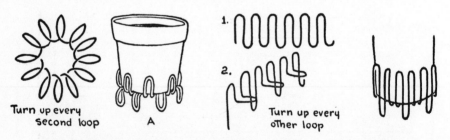

Turn up every second loop   A   1.   2.   Turn up every other loop

LOOPED-WIRE FLOWER POT HOLDERS. Many different kinds of flower-pot holders can be made of wire—so many that we can illustrate only a few. The looped-wire holders shown here are two of the most popular and easy to make. They can be made of coat-hanger wire or ¹⁄₁₆-inch or thinner soft iron wire. These holders can also be used to hold glasses or dishes.

FLOWER POT ARBOR. This is a little indoor arbor to put on a shelf or table. It can be painted white, the usual color for outdoor arbors, or black to suit the wrought-iron mode of today. You can use $\frac{1}{16}$-inch or lighter wire for the framework of the arbor and the fence, with thinner wire for the crosspieces.

Coffee can

PLANT POLES AND TRELLISES. These plant climbers and trellises may be used with potted house plants. They are made of soft iron wire and painted black or in bright colors. The smaller ones are for use with plants or vines planted in flower pots or dishes, while the larger ones are for ivy or other climbing plants, planted in larger containers. All are quite easy to put together and the drawings give the essential details of their construction. The wire flowers can be dipped in liquid plastic and then painted.

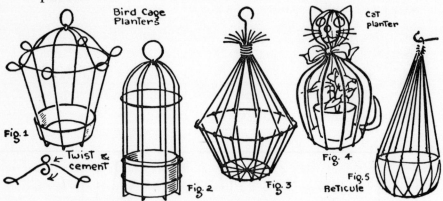

PLANTERS. Planters have become increasingly popular. When filled with trailing ivy or arrangements of small flowers they add a distinctive accent to any room. They are designed, as a rule, to hold flower bowls or dishes, rather than flower pots.

The construction details of the bird-cage planters are simple, but time and patience are required to put the wire pieces together symmetrically. Soft iron wire and brass wire are commonly used in cage planters, and both look very attractive. Note that the flower receptacle must be put inside the cage before the wire pieces are fastened together around it.

The construction of the reticule planter is difficult to describe, but the drawing should make it clear. The extra wires added near the bottom to form the mesh are twisted around the main wires and the twists are then reinforced with cement. This planter is very attractive when made of copper or brass wire. Different sizes of wire can be used, depending on the size and weight of the flower bowl to be used.

The cat planter takes a little time to put together. The construction is not difficult if you go slowly and follow the drawing. It is a good idea to make a wire-solder model first to measure the lengths of the stiffer wire pieces needed. This planter has an open bottom so that it can be placed over a plant set in a bowl.

PUSHCART PLANT HOLDER. This little push-cart is designed to hold a ten-cent-store metal box for plants or flowers. It is made of $\frac{1}{16}$-inch or slightly thinner iron wire. The main framework is bent from a single piece of wire. Crosspieces and the V-shaped support at the front end are then cemented to it. The spokes of the wheels consist of two pieces of wire bent as shown and cemented in place.

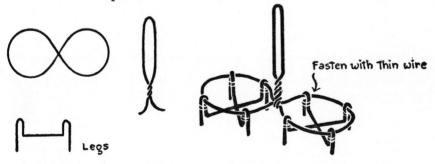

Fasten with Thin wire

Legs

SALT AND PEPPER HOLDERS. The salt and pepper holder shown in the drawing is made of $\frac{1}{16}$-inch or thinner soft iron wire. One piece of wire is bent to form a figure 8, the circles being of the size required for the salt and pepper shakers for which the holder is intended. This piece is cemented and wired at the center. The handle is then made, and its lower end is twisted and cemeted to the center of the figure 8. Cross wires with right-angle bends near each end are placed over the framework, the loops pinched tight with pliers, and wound tight with fine wire or cemented to the figure 8.

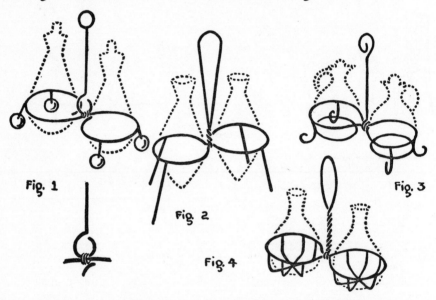

Fig. 1   Fig. 2   Fig. 3   Fig. 4

OIL AND VINEGAR CRUETS. Use $\frac{1}{16}$-inch soft iron wire or copper wire for these cruets. They are quite easy to make, and the drawings show the main details of each one's construction. The different pieces that make up each cruet are fastened together with cement or with twisted wire coated with cement.

MINIATURE FURNITURE. Wire is a wonderful material with which to make some kinds of miniature furniture. Any kind of thin wire can be used. Florist's wire is excellent, and wire solder is well worth a try.

The seat of a chair can be made of a wire frame and wire crosspieces, or may be of wood. Table tops may be made of wood or of a wire frame with thin wire cross-

pieces cemented to it. Cement and tape can be used to join pieces together. Cemented-on scraps of fabric provide realistic-looking upholstery.

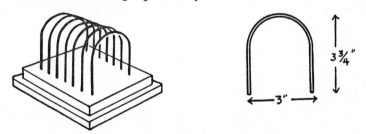

TOAST RACK. The base of this rack consists of two squares of ⅜-inch thick wood. The lower piece is 5½ inches square, and the upper piece 5 inches square.

Cement the two pieces together and then drill ½-inch deep holes ⅝ inch apart to hold the wire hoops. Use ¹⁄₁₆-inch or slightly heavier wire for the hoops, and drill the holes to fit the thickness of the wire. Bend the seven hoops on a simple wooden jig of the kind described in CHAPTER ONE. Each hoop is 3¾ inches high and 3 inches wide. When the hoops are ready, cement them into the holes in the base.

NAPKIN DOLL. This wire manikin holds a dozen paper or cloth napkins, which form her swirling skirt. They are held in place by passing a rubber band or a wire circle around their tops.

The doll is about 10½ inches high and is made of ⅟₁₆-inch to ⅛-inch wire, with a button or large bead for a face. The base may be of coiled wire or of wood or plastic. You can leave the wire body and arms uncovered and can paint them, or you can dress the upper part of the doll in a blouse made from scraps of silk or rayon.

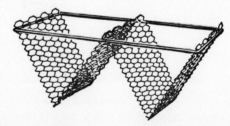

CHICKEN-WIRE MAGAZINE RACK. To make this magazine rack, get a 36-inch width of chicken wire at a hardware store and bend it to form a letter W. Bend

over any rough edges and then run a length of ⅛-inch
or 3⁄16-inch soft iron wire through the top. Hardware
cloth may be used instead of chicken wire.

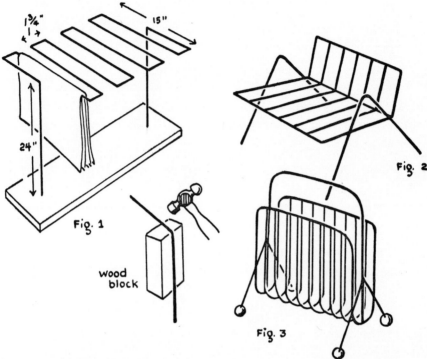

Fig. 1

wood block

Fig. 2

Fig. 3

MAGAZINE RACKS. Here are three different kinds
of magazine racks, all interesting to make. Use ¼-inch
iron wire, or even ⅜-inch, to give sufficient strength.

The stand in Fig. 1 requires a total of 15 feet, 3 inches
of wire, which allows an inch for the ends that are inserted in ½-inch-deep holes in the wooden base. Use 6-
gauge iron wire, since heavier wire is difficult to bend to
the required shapes. This thickness of wire usually comes
in 10-foot or 20-foot lengths. Cut the wire so the joins
between the two or three pieces used will come at a right-
angle corner. The joins can then be reinforced by the
use of a right-angle or L-shaped metal bracket, as described
in CHAPTER ONE.

Make a full-scale drawing on the top of the rack, using

the dimensions shown in Fig. 1. Measure on the wire where each bend is to come, marking the place with a file. Cut a block of wood 1¾ inches wide to serve as a jig. Then make the bends, using the block of wood and a hammer to tap each bend to its final shape. Check the wire against the drawing as you go along as an aid to getting each bend in the right place.

You can use ¼-inch wire for the rack in Fig. 2, which contains no difficult bends. The rack consists of two end pieces, a framework for the bottom and back, and five right-angle pieces. The base of the center framework should measure about 14 by 11 inches to hold the largest size popular magazines.

Fasten the end pieces to the center framework with cement or solder, and add twisted wire if it seems necessary. Fasten the right-angle pieces to the framework by bending over their ends and pinching the bends tight with a hammer.

The framework of the rack in Fig. 3 may be made of either ¼-inch or ³⁄₁₆-inch wire. The rack consists of two end pieces, a curved center framework, and eight curved wires. The handle is optional. The center framework should be about 14½ inches long, and should be curved (using a jig), so that the opening at the top is about 7 inches wide. Use the fastening methods suggested for the rack in Fig. 2.

BOOK RACKS. Both of these book racks are made of ⅛-inch to ³⁄₁₆-inch soft iron wire painted black, or of brass wire of the same size.

The legs of the rack shown in Fig. 1 are bent at right angles and can be tipped with wooden balls or rubber tips. Each side of each leg is 5½ inches long, so a wire 11 inches long is needed. The ends of the trough are also bent at right angles, each side being 6 inches long. The entire trough is made from a single piece of wire. A rack

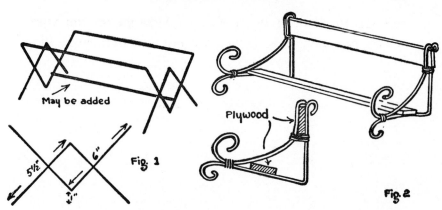

13 inches long requires a piece of wire with a total length of 50 inches. Join the ends by one of the methods described in CHAPTER ONE. An additional wire may be added to the lower part of the back of the rack, though it is not entirely necessary.

The book rack shown in Fig. 2 is made of four pieces of wire, which form the end pieces, and two pieces of plywood or hardboard. Suggested dimensions are 12 inches long by 6 inches high.

Make a full-scale drawing of one of the end pieces. Then bend the wire to shape, checking it against the drawing as you proceed with the bending. Fasten the two wire parts of each end together with cement and add twisted wire if it seems necessary. Then join the ends by cementing to them the two strips of plywood or hardboard, and paint the entire rack black.

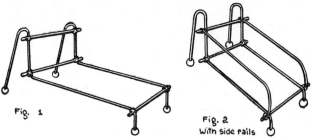

RECORD RACK. This rack can be made to fit either 10-inch or 12-inch records. It is made from 3⁄16-inch or

¼-inch iron wire painted black. The framework consists of two pieces bent to form the front and back legs and the sides of the bottom. These are joined by three crosspieces as shown. Side rails can be added, if you wish, to keep the records from slipping off sideways.

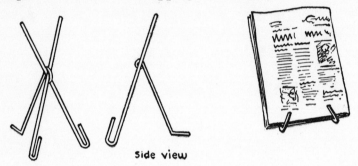

Side view

READING RACK. This rack will hold newspapers or magazines and is especially useful to breakfast-table readers. A smaller size can be made to fit a book.

The rack can be made of ⅟₁₆-inch or heavier iron wire. All three pieces are curved with pliers at one end. The two crosspieces are wired together and the wire is then coated with cement. The top end of the prop is then bent around the center of the X and clamped tight with pliers, and the rack is painted black.

BOOK ENDS. Wire book ends of the conventional type are easy to make, and it is fun to decorate them with different kinds of bent wire designs. Some suggested patterns are shown in the drawings.

Use ⅟₁₆-inch or heavier iron or other wire. Iron wire

is usually painted black, while copper, brass or aluminum wire is left unpainted. The frame of each end is made from one piece of wire, which is bent to shape as shown.

For the little seated figure, use three pieces of ⅟₁₆-inch steel or iron wire—one for the body, one for the arms, and one for the legs. Cement the pieces together. Use a colored wooden ball for the head, and pieces of thin sheet metal or cardboard for the book.

WALL SHELF. For this shelf use ⅛-inch or heavier soft iron wire for the main framework, and ⅟₁₆-inch or slightly thinner wire for the bottom rods that run between the two end frames.

Make a full-scale drawing of one end frame to serve as a guide. Before starting to bend each frame, twist a circle in the end of the wire to take a nail or screw. The two lengthwise wires that join the tops of the end frames are cemented in place *beneath* the top wires of the end pieces. Then they are further secured with twisted wire, which enables them to bear any weight put on the shelf. The shelf may be of wood, plastic or cork. A block of cork looks particularly well with black-painted wire.

FISH SHELF. The main parts of the fish shelf are made of ⅛-inch or ³⁄₁₆-inch soft iron wire painted black. Use thinner wire for the little fish at the top. Shape both with pliers or with a simple bending jig. Cement or solder the pieces together and, since there will be a strain on the two main uprights, it is as well to be on the safe side by fastening them with twisted wire in addition. Use a wooden shelf **or** a ten-cent-store metal-lace shelf, and cement it to the two horizontal rods.

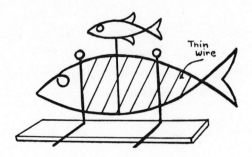

ALL-WIRE SHELVES AND STANDS. All-wire shelves of the kind shown in the drawings are easy enough to make, but they do require a good deal of time and patience. For most large pieces of this type use ¼-inch soft iron-wire rod for the heavier parts and ³⁄₁₆-inch or ⅛-inch wire for the lighter parts. The standing shelves can be made large enough to stand on the floor and hold magazines or records. But articles of the same design can also be made of lighter wire and small enough to stand on a desk or table.

The stand in Fig. 1 can be used for magazines or flowers and, with the addition of the two upright frames to the lower shelf, it becomes a record holder. It can also be used as a telephone table or a hostess server for parties. Suggested dimensions are 27 inches long, 16 inches wide and 22 inches high.

Bend the two end frames together to make them identical. The ends of the two tray sections rest on and are cemented to crosspieces of ¼-inch wire. The crosspieces are fastened in place with cement or solder and, for extra security, you can cement and wire beneath each end of each crosspiece a vertical wire prop or support, as shown in the drawings.

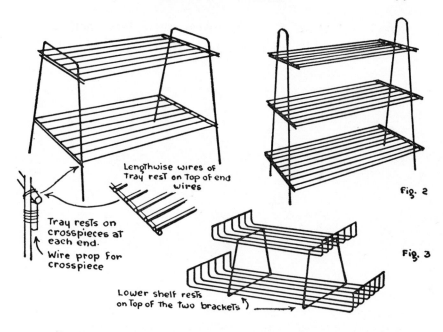

Lengthwise wires of
Tray rest on Top of end
wires

Tray rests on
crosspieces at
each end.

Wire prop for
crosspiece

Lower shelf rests
on Top of the two brackets

Fig. 2

Fig. 3

In making the tray sections it is best to have the length-wise wires rest on top of the ends of the frames. If this is done, there will be ample strength to bear any normal weight. You can also use ready-made grills for shelves, painting them black.

Fig. 2 shows a three-tiered stand made in the same way as Fig. 1.

The wall shelf in Fig. 3 is in modern wrought-iron design and will hold books or knickknacks. It can be hung to the wall on hooks, in which case the supporting brackets had better be rectangles and both shelves of the same width. Use ¼-inch iron wire for the two brackets and for the crosspieces at the ends of the upper and lower shelves. Use ⅛-inch wire for the lengthwise rods.

Fasten the top shelf to the top of the two brackets with cement and twisted wire. This will give ample strength. The bottom shelf rests on the bottom bars of the two brackets.

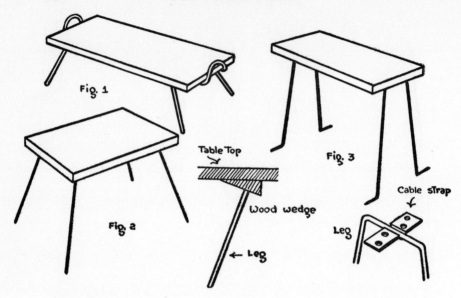

Fig. 1

Fig. 3

Fig. 2

Table Top

Wood wedge

← Leg

Cable strap

Leg

TABLES. All the tables shown in the drawings are made on the same principle, with easily bent wire legs fastened to a wooden top. Tables made in this way can be of any size and height. The drawings show only a few examples.

Use ³⁄₁₆-inch to ⅜-inch soft iron-wire rod for the legs and bend the legs in pairs in order to make them identical. The legs are fastened to the under side of the table top with cable straps or strips of sheet metal. Cable straps, designed to hold electrical cable, can be purchased at hardware and electrical supply stores. Wood wedges can be screwed to the table top and the legs fastened to them in order to give the legs an outward splay.

EASY-TO-MAKE UTILITY TABLES. The base and top of these tables consist of two circles sawed from 1-inch board. The base is 7 inches in diameter and the top has a 6-inch diameter. Three ¼-inch holes, arranged in an equilateral triangle, are drilled in the base and top. Three lengths of ¼-inch iron wire are then cemented into the holes. The table should be about 24 inches high. When completed, the base and top are given two coats of var-

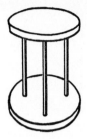

nish or are painted red or some other color. The wire rods are painted black.

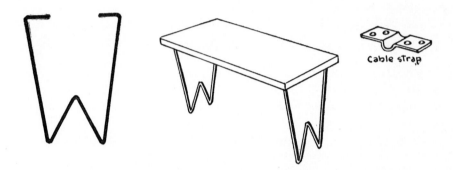

cable strap

W-TYPE TABLE LEGS. The legs of these tables are bent to the shape shown in the drawing, and can be of varying heights to make different kinds of tables. The tops of the wire are bent inward, so the legs can be fastened to the under side of the table top with strips of sheet metal or cable straps (which are designed to hold electrical cable and can be purchased at hardware stores). Use ³⁄₁₆-inch to ⅜-inch soft iron-wire rod for the legs, depending on the size of the table and the weight it will have to bear.

WASTEBASKETS. To make the wastebasket shown in Fig. 1, four legs of ⅛-inch soft iron wire are hooked over the top of a black-painted circular basket and the hooks are pinched tightly in place with pliers. Cement may be used to secure them to the basket's sides, but this is usually not necessary. Twelve pieces of ⅛-inch wire, bent at each end, are then put in place, three of them going

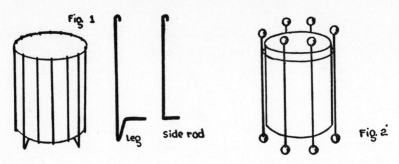

between each pair of legs. When all the pieces are in place, paint them yellow or red.

The basket in Fig. 2 rests inside a framework made of ⅛-inch iron wire. The side rods are cemented at top and bottom into holes drilled in plastic or wooden balls. This arrangement is very striking when the basket is painted red and the wires black.

FENCE-WIRE SCREENS. Screens are made by nailing or stapling fence wire to hinged wooden frames. Possibly you can dig up an old, unused screen in the attic, which will provide the framework. Fasten fence wire, obtained at a hardware store, to the screen. Record-album covers can be cemented to the wire for decoration, or colored reproductions of paintings may be used.

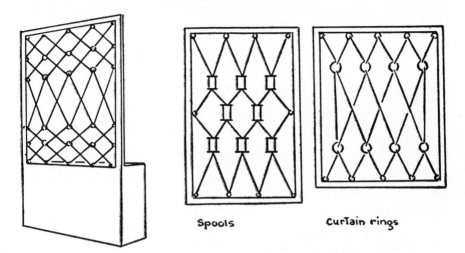

Spools   Curtain rings

ROOM DIVIDER. This can be made quite simply from four pieces of lumber strung with a wire design. The wire may be soft iron, steel or copper, and ⅟₁₆ inch is a good size for most dividers. Different sizes of wire can be used, depending upon the size of the divider. The wire is passed through screw eyes, curtain rings or wooden drapery rings and the ends are twisted into the rings.

Three pieces of wire will make the pattern shown—two diagonals and a diamond in the center. You can also use such things as curtain rings or painted spools as part of a divider pattern. Iron or steel wire may be painted any color you desire after the divider is completed.

CHAPTER THREE

WIRE JEWELRY AND ACCESSORIES

eeeeeeeeeeeeeeeeeeeeeeeee

Most wire jewelry is made of 20-gauge, 18-gauge and 14-gauge copper wire. Aluminum, brass, silver and gold wire are also used, though less commonly, largely because they are more expensive.

Twist or bend the wire to the various shapes required, using your fingers and small smooth-jawed, flat-nosed pliers or sometimes small round-nosed pliers. Bending jigs are also used. The principal kinds of jigs are illustrated in CHAPTER ONE.

After bending, it is often necessary to pound a piece in order to flatten it. To do this place the piece on top of several layers of newspaper and pound it with a small wooden mallet or the heel of a shoe. Do not use a metal hammer, since it will mark the wire.

A widely used method of finishing wire jewelry is to lacquer it with clear nail polish. A more professional method is to use liver of sulphur, which you can get at a drugstore.

There are a number of steps in a thorough finishing job. First, scrub the jewelry piece, using warm water, soap and a soft brush. Then dip it in a solution made with half a cup of warm water and a piece of liver of sulphur about the size of a lump of sugar. Next rinse the piece in cold water to remove some of the black deposited by the solution.

The next step is to "antique" or oxidize the piece in order to give the wire a subdued and more attractive coloring. This is done with dental pumice, obtainable at a drugstore. Wet your thumb, dip it into the pumice, and rub it over the wire to remove more of the black. You can remove as much of the black as you like, stopping when the wire looks the way you want it to. When you reach this point, rinse the piece in warm water and, with a brush, remove all the pumice.

When the piece has dried polish it with a hand buffer on which some jeweler's rouge has been rubbed. The buffer may be homemade, consisting of a piece of white felt glued to a flat stick about 1 inch wide and 10 inches long. Jeweler's rouge, together with jeweler's lacquer and thinner for the lacquer, which are used in the next step, can be obtained at a jewelry store. Jeweler's lacquer keeps copper from turning dark.

After polishing the piece with jeweler's rouge, scrub it with soap and hot water to remove all traces of the rouge. This is the final step with a piece of jewelry made of silver. Do not lacquer silver, since the lacquer turns it yellow.

For a copper piece, prepare lacquer by mixing in a jar one part of jeweler's lacquer with two parts of lacquer thinner. Using a bent-wire hook, dip the piece in the mixture for a few seconds. Let the wire dry and after four hours dip it in the lacquer again. Then let the piece dry for 12 hours.

SPIRAL-COIL JEWELRY. This is one of the easiest kinds of coiled-wire jewelry to make. Use 16-gauge or 18-gauge copper or silver wire.

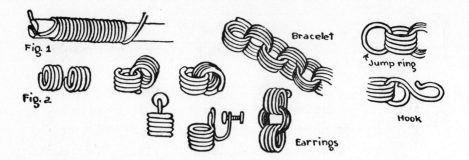

The wire is wound around a pencil as shown in the drawing. When you have covered most of the pencil, remove the coiled wire and cut it into short sections. Each section contains four complete rounds or circles of the wire. To cut the wire easily, bend each section away from the rest of the coil.

For a bracelet you will need about 22 sections. When these have all been coiled and cut, they are joined together by the method shown in the drawings. The end of one section is passed down through the center of another section. The first section is then wound through the other one, by turning it around and around.

When the bracelet is long enough, make a jump ring—a single circle—of 14-gauge wire and insert it through one of the end sections. Make a hook of 14-gauge wire and insert it in the other end section. Then lacquer the entire bracelet with clear nail polish or the finish described in the introduction to this section.

A necklace is made in exactly the same way, but is of course much longer. Earrings are made by cementing one or more four-circle sections to earrings backs.

COILED-WIRE JEWELRY. The bracelets, necklaces and matching earrings shown in the drawings are sometimes called Egyptian, because a similar kind of jewelry was made of wire in Egypt about 2,000 B.C.

Use 18-gauge or 20-gauge copper wire. Each bracelet

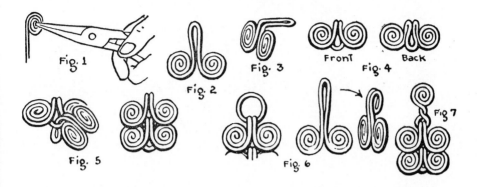

Fig. 1 Fig. 2 Fig. 3 Front Fig. 4 Back Fig. 5 Fig. 6 Fig 7

or necklace consists of a series of sections or links, and the first step is to make up a series of sections equal to the desired length of the finished piece. Each section is formed with long-nosed pliers from a piece of wire 6 inches long.

Using the long-nosed pliers, make the concentric circles in each end of each piece as shown. Then bend a loop in the center of each piece of wire (Fig. 2). It is a good idea to make a full-sized drawing of one section to serve as a guide. Place each section on the drawing as it is nearing completion. This will help to make all the sections identical.

When all the sections are made, place each one on top of several layers of newspaper and pound it with a small wooden mallet to flatten and stiffen it.

Then, using the pliers, bend down the loop of each section until it forms a right angle (Fig. 3). Next push the loop down flat against the coils, using your fingers (Fig. 4).

The sections are then linked together by inserting the loop of one section down through the loop of another section, as in Fig. 5. Pinch the loop of the section you have added, until it is flat against the first section (Fig. 5).

When you have joined enough sections to make the piece the desired length, add a hook to one end and a jump ring to the opposite end (Fig. 6). The hook is best made by a coiled section similar to the other sections but with a much longer length of wire between the two coils. This length is then bent over to form the hook. The jump ring is made by winding wire around a pencil to form a circle. After it has been inserted, turn it so that the joint is inside the loop of the section to which it has been added.

When a bracelet or necklace is completed, lacquer it with clear nail polish or apply a finish as described above.

Matching earrings are easy to make and are assembled as shown in Fig. 7.

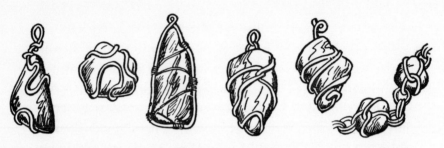

WIRED STONE JEWELRY. Rough uncut gems set in unconventional wrappings of wire are a very popular type of jewelry. Gold and silver wire is used by commercial jewelers; but amateurs can achieve striking effects with copper, brass or even shiny galvanized steel wire. Uncut gems of all kinds and at all prices—many of them very low—can be obtained from dealers who advertise in the craft and hobby magazines.

Examples of this type of work suitable for earrings, bracelet charms, necklace pendants and pins are shown in the drawings. There are no set rules to follow in devising this kind of jewelry. You are your own designer and can work out any attractive or unusual patterns that appeal to you.

WIRE AND PLASTIC SIGNATURE JEWELRY. It is easy to make handsome and unusual jewelry novelties such as pins, earrings and key chain tags by embedding thin wire between two pieces of clear plastic. It is best

Pin

charm   Earrings

Monogram Pins

to use quite fine wire, such as 24-gauge or thinner copper wire.

Use two pieces of acrylic plastic such as Lucite or Plexiglas, each half as thick as the finished piece is to be. Bend the wire to form the signature or initials, and place it on one piece of plastic. Cover it with clear cement, put the second piece of plastic on top, and leave the two pieces clamped together for about twelve hours. After the cement has hardened, trim the plastic to size and polish the edges. Cement pins to pinbacks, and drill a small hole in each key-chain tag for the chain.

If the plastic pieces do not join closely enough, because of the thickness of the wire, heat one piece of the plastic to a pliable condition and press the wire into it before cementing the other piece in place. The heating can be done in an oven.

Wire signatures, initials and monograms can also be cemented to a single piece of plastic or of mother-of-pearl, to make attractive pins and bracelet charms.

EARRINGS AND PINS. There is no limit to the different kinds of earrings and matching pins that you can make with wire. Many of these pieces can also be hung on chains to serve as pendants. The drawings give an idea of the many possibilities.

All of the pieces shown are made by bending copper or silver wire—usually 14 gauge or 18 gauge. Some of the pieces need cement. In some cases, you may wish to use a bead, button or artificial pearl and cement the end or

ends of the wire into it, or simply to use as an ornament. In other pieces, the wire should be flattened a little by placing it on several thicknesses of newspaper and pounding it gently with a wooden mallet.

FLOWER PINS. The drawings show several kinds of twisted-wire flower pins. The designs are so interesting and out of the ordinary that they do not need paint to add to their attractiveness. The sheen of copper, brass, silver or even galvanized steel wire is sufficient to make a very decorative pin. Sometimes jewelry of this kind is painted dull black or the color of unpainted soft iron wire. When the flowers are completed, they are wired to safety pins or are fastened to commercial pinbacks with cement or wire. Single flowers or clusters can be used.

HAIR BANDS AND CLIPS. Gleaming hair bands of several different designs can be made from springy steel, copper, brass or silver wire. The drawings show several

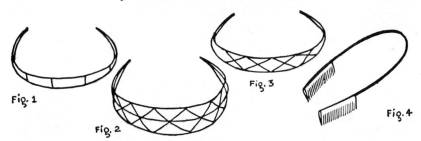

Fig. 1

Fig. 2

Fig. 3

Fig. 4

types of bands, which can be worn by themselves, or trimmed with ribbons, flowers or scarves.

In making the bands shown in Figs. 1, 2 and 3, it is best to twist together the ends of the main framework wires to make a secure fastening. Then cover the twists with small bits of ribbon to keep the wires from tangling with the hair. The other wires can be fastened in place either with cement or by twisting them around the framework wires. The comb clip is simply a single piece of springy wire with curved side combs cemented and wired to its ends.

Bead or button

Bead

Cork

Thin wire

BIRD LAPEL ORNAMENTS. Wire can be twisted into different kinds of bird outlines, which make interesting and colorful lapel ornaments. The birds are cemented or fastened with twisted wire to safety pins or commercial pinbacks. In some cases, beads, buttons or artificial gems are used for heads or eyes or bodies.

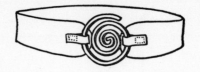

SPIRAL BELT BUCKLES. Spiral belt buckles, sometimes called swirl buckles, are expandable, the one shown in the drawing expanding from about 1½ inches to 3 inches. For this buckle you will need 16 inches of 8-gauge (about ⅛-inch) copper wire.

To make the buckle, cut a 16-inch length of the wire and file both ends round. Then bend the wire into a spiral, using pliers to make the first sharp bend and your fingers for the rest. Apply a finish when the buckle is completed. The buckle will fit the turned-back ends of a cloth, leather or plastic belt, or can be attached to a wider belt as shown in the drawing, and can be turned around in order to move the ends of the belt closer or farther apart.

center

WIRE AND PLASTIC POINSETTIA. These are made of copper wire petals dipped in liquid plastic and painted red. To make one, cut eight pieces of 18-gauge or 20-gauge copper wire, each about 10 inches long. Twist each piece around a piece of dowel to form a circle, using one-half the length for each circle. The remainder of the wire is for stem. With your fingers or pliers pull out the circles to form five petals and three leaves.

Dip each piece in liquid plastic, withdrawing it slowly. The plastic will form a skin or film over the open space of each piece. Stick each piece in a block of clay to dry for about two hours. Then apply plastic lacquer paint— red for the petals and green for the leaves.

When the paint is dry, assemble the flower. Tie two petals together with thin wire. Bind another petal to these, and then add the fourth and fifth petals. Twist green binding tape around the wire stem of each petal and of each leaf. Then arrange the leaves and petals as you want them, and bind all the stems together with green tape.

CHAPTER FOUR

COAT-HANGER CRAFT

llllllllllllllllllllllll

This wire is tough and springy and hard to bend properly with your fingers. But with pliers, a hammer and bending jigs, you can make it do almost anything you wish.

To make this wire much easier to bend and shape build a small bonfire, put a number of hangers in it, and let them stay there for fifteen minutes or more. When you remove them, let them cool and then clean them with steel wool.

Here are some of the many things you can make and do with coat-hanger wire.

COAT-HANGER TWISTS. The figures shown in the drawings were made on the spur of the moment by guests at a coat-hanger party given by an editor of *Popular Science Monthly*. None of the guests had ever before tried their hand at making things with coat hangers, but they came up with some interesting results.

The work was done with pliers, hammers, tin shears, soldering equipment and a bending jig of the kind illustrated. This jig was made by driving three nails into a block of wood, two of them close together, and the third a couple of inches away to provide leverage. (This material is used here with the permission of *Popular Science Monthly* and is copyright, 1955, by Popular Science Publishing Co., Inc.).

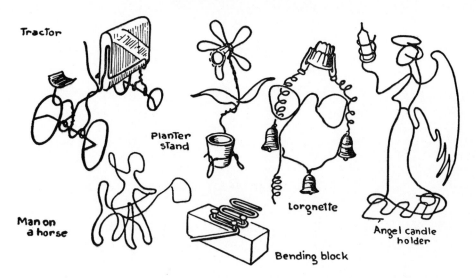

Tractor

Planter stand

Man on a horse

Lorgnette

Bending block

Angel candle holder

CANDLE HOLDERS. The drawings show several kinds of candle holders that are easy to make with coat-hanger wire and a pair of pliers. The hanging holder is made from two hangers, wired together at top and bottom, with the candle socket cemented or soldered in place. The drawings show the construction of the other holders. Their candle sockets are made of coat-hanger wire bent to the required shape and cemented to pieces of wood, plastic or metal.

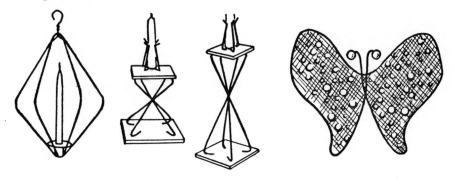

COAT-HANGER BUTTERFLY. A few easy bends will quickly change a coat hanger into a butterfly that makes an excellent wall decoration. Cut off the hook and then bend the wire with pliers to the shape shown in the drawing. Cement wire screening to the wings, and cement two beads or buttons to the antennãe. The screening can be decorated with sparkling sequins or beads, if you wish, to add some brilliant spots of color.

BROOM HOLDER. A piece of twisted coat-hanger wire or soft iron wire makes a simple but effective device for holding a broom. The wire is twisted as shown in the drawing and is fastened to the wall with two screw eyes. The small turn on the left end of the straight part holds the hook out far enough from the wall to make it easy to place the broom in the hook. The weight of the broom keeps it in position.

HANDY HOOKS. These hooks are handy in clothes closets for holding purses, umbrellas or belts. They will hold cleaning brushes in the broom closet, freshly ironed clothes in the laundry. In a garage they can be used for garden tools, and in a child's room for clothes and toys.

The hooks are made by bending clothes hangers to the shape shown and then snipping off the extra wire. Small rubber tips or plastic or wooden balls can be cemented to the ends of the wire.

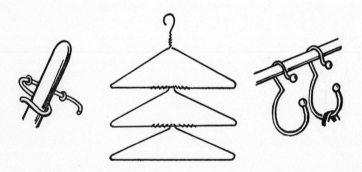

CLOSET STRETCHER. By joining four or five coat hangers as shown in the drawing you can quickly make a space-saving gadget which will hold a number of garments on one hook. Cut the hook off one hanger and untwist the wire at the base of the hook. Slip this hanger over the bar of another hanger and retwist the wire. Then bend the twisted wire down to one side. Add other hangers in the same way.

COAT-HANGER HAT HOLDER. A coat hanger bent to form a circular loop as shown in the drawing makes a hat holder which will keep a man's hat from getting out of shape. Such a hanger can also be used as a rack for ties or towels.

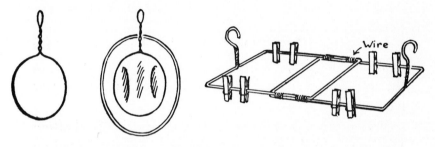

DOUBLE-BAR DRIER. A double-bar hanger can often be a great convenience, particularly if you are cramped for space. Such a hanger is made from two wire hangers. They are bent with pliers to the shape shown in the drawing and are fastened together with twisted wire. Hangers of this kind are usually used with clip clothespins which hold hose, gloves and other articles that are being dried.

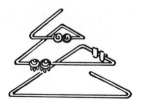

EARRING HOLDER. This is a neat, little earring holder that can be bent to shape very quickly. You can use coat-hanger wire or any other kind of fairly stiff $\frac{1}{16}$-inch wire. Use a piece about 14 inches long and bend it with pliers to the shape shown. Make sure that the base is flat, so the holder will stand firmly upright. Complete the holder by covering the wire with ribbon, colored tape or velvet.

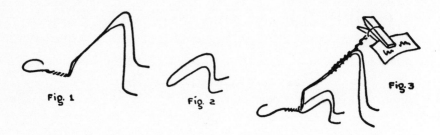

DOG MEMO HOLDER. This pooch who holds notes or memos in his mouth can be made of a coat hanger, as the drawings show, or, in a smaller version, of iron or copper wire.

If you use a coat hanger, start by cutting its bottom wire in two at the center. Making the hook the curled-up tail of the dog, bend up the slanting side wires just below the hook to make the animal's back. Then bend up the ends of the two wires to form the front feet (Fig. 1).

Cut off a section of another coat hanger and bend it to the shape shown in Fig. 2, to make the hind legs. Wire this piece to the body, close to the tail, as in Fig. 3. Then twist on a short piece of wire to form the neck. Bend over the top of the neck and wire to it the head, which is a spring clothespin. When the dog is completed, you can tie a ribbon bow around his neck.

CHAPTER FIVE

CHRISTMAS DECORATIONS

Wire Christmas ornaments can be made in a number of different forms. Coat-hanger wire can be used for large pieces and much thinner copper and galvanized steel wire for smaller ones. All the ornaments are made by twisting or cementing together the pieces of wire needed for their construction. The drawings indicate clearly how each ornament is made.

The gleam of copper wire and shiny steel wire gives a very Christmasy appearance by itself. Coat-hanger wire can be painted in bright colors or wrapped with ribbon. Wire can also be sprayed with glitter or artificial snow, both of which can be obtained at ten-cent stores.

CHRISTMAS ANGELS. These angels are designed to be bent to shape, using thin, easily handled wire, and cemented to a cardboard or heavy colored paper background. They are interesting experiments in careful decorative bending work and, when made of copper wire or silvery steel wire and mounted on blue or red backgrounds, are exceptionally pretty.

CHRISTMAS SLEIGH AND REINDEER. A Santa-Claus sleigh and reindeer make a fine Christmas centerpiece or mantel decoration. You can put a toy Santa Claus in the sleigh, or fill it with candy, fruit or Christmas-tree ornaments.

All the pieces are easy to bend to the required shapes, using $\frac{1}{16}$-inch or thinner wire. Suggested dimensions for the sleigh are 10½ inches long by 5½ inches wide. For such a sleigh the reindeer should be about 7 inches long. The different wire parts are cemented together. The seat part of the sleigh can be made from hardware cloth, if you wish. If you do not use hardware cloth, you can make the sleigh as shown and line it with red construction paper, cardboard or cloth.

CHRISTMAS-CANDLE TREE. The base of this candle tree is a circle made of ⅛-inch to ³⁄₁₆-inch soft iron wire to which four candle brackets are cemented. The brackets may be purchased at a hardware or ten-cent store, or may be made at home by cementing short lengths of plastic or metal tubing to disks of plastic or thin sheet metal. The tree consists of two pieces of wire bent to shape and fastened to the base with cement and twisted wire. The wires that form the tree are twisted together at the top. The legs are pieces of fairly heavy wire bent over at the top and hooked to the base. The hooks are pinched tight with pliers.

CHRISTMAS ANGEL. This Christmas angel is designed to be made of thin copper or other wire, such as 18 gauge to 22 gauge, and mounted on a background of white or colored paper. Admittedly, it is a design that requires a good deal of time and patience to put together and is intended only for genuine wirecraft enthusiasts. Actually, the design consists chiefly of pieces of looped wire, and the loops are easy to make if you use a bending jig.

SLEIGH PENDANT. A Santa-Claus sleigh filled with pine branches and pine cones or with colored Christmas-tree balls makes an attractive and unusual Christmas decoration. It may be stood on a mantel or table, and can be suspended from the ceiling. The framework of the sleigh is made of $\frac{1}{16}$-inch soft iron wire or from coat-hanger wire, and the interior scrolls are of thinner wire. The parts are cemented together; and the wires at the front, where the runners meet the body of the sleigh, are fastened together with twisted wire coated with cement.

Line sleigh with hardware wire or with red and silver paper.

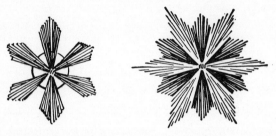

CHRISTMAS STAR. This star needs a good many pieces of wire, but the final effect is well worth the time involved. It is modeled after the traditional stars made of straw which are used in Sweden at Christmastime. Use thin copper wire, shiny galvanized steel wire, or a combination of both. Make a cardboard circle to serve as the center, and cement the inner ends of the wire to it. This eliminates the overlapping that would occur if all the wires crossed each other at the center. A wire ring is used as part of the design, and is cemented to the back of the star when all the other wires have been put in place.

SANTA CLAUS OUTLINE FIGURES. The drawings show how Santa Claus can be reproduced very realistically in wire, which is bent to the required shapes and cemented to a colored-paper background. Copper wire or shiny galvanized steel wire and red paper are perhaps the best choice.

CHRISTMAS GREETING. Since letters can be formed so easily by bending flexible wire, and because of wire's Christmasy glitter and gleam, you can use wire to make Christmas greeting pieces. Fasten to a big piece of red construction paper—or red ribbon, the words "Merry Christmas" spelled out in wire. If you use paper, cement the wire to it. If you use ribbon, fasten the writing in place with thread.

MINIATURE CHRISTMAS TREES. The easiest way to make these trees stand up is to "plant" them in earth or in rolled-up corrugated board in small flower pots or other containers. They can also be stapled to wooden bases, or their trunks can be cemented into holes drilled in wood or plastic bases. The natural sheen of copper or steel wire makes attractive trees, but the wire may also be painted green or sprayed with glitter or artificial snow.

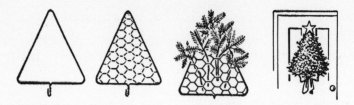

CHICKEN-WIRE CHRISTMAS TREE. This is a novel kind of Christmas tree, which is designed to be hung on the front door, on a wall, or on the doors of rooms inside the house.

The tree is made with a coat hanger, a 12-inch by 15-inch piece of chicken wire, some fine steel or iron wire, and some short Christmas-tree boughs, ranging from 6 to 12 inches long.

Bend the hanger into a Christmas-tree shape, using the handle for the trunk. Then cover the frame with chicken wire, fastening it in place with the fine wire. Weave in the boughs, so they lie fairly flat. Make the top bough stand straight up to form the top of the tree. Then weave in a few boughs on a slant to form the shape of the tree's top. Next weave in two bottom boughs, one on either side, to form a base properly proportioned to the height of the tree.

Continue by weaving in the rest of the boughs, working from the bottom to the top. Keep the boughs flat and slightly overlapping. As you put them in place, tie them in position with thin wire. When the tree is completed, hang it up and then trim it with tinsel and Christmas-tree ornaments, including a star at the top of the tree, and tie a red ribbon bow around the trunk.

CHAPTER SIX

FIGURES, FRAMES, FLOWERS

WALL DECORATIONS. You can make dozens of different kinds of wall decorations with wire. Wire of many kinds and sizes can be used, including coat-hanger wire, the thickness of the wire depending on the size of the decoration. Plastic-covered electrical wire is popular with some craftsmen, because it is large and easy to bend but holds its shape. The wire can be painted black or other colors or, in the case of gleaming copper, brass or aluminum wire, can be left unpainted.

The decorations may be large or small, depending on the wall space you want them to occupy. Stylized fish and bird and animal figures are popular, as are abstract designs.

Varied lighting produces interesting three-dimensional silhouettes when wire decorations are hung with spacers (short bits of wood or wire), that hold them about ½ inch from the wall. Parts of the decorations may be covered with screen wire or perforated sheet metal to create different effects.

When making some wall-decoration figures, you may find it helpful to thumbtack the different pieces, as they are bent to shape, to a board. This helps to line the figure up, and also to hold the pieces in place after you have applied cement.

WIRE AND BEAD CORSAGES. Wire and glass bead corsages are fun to make and some people have developed a money-making hobby in them.

The corsages are made with jeweler's wire, glass beads and glass leaves which can be purchased at hobby shops or from firms that sell artificial flower supplies. Start with a piece of wire about 12 inches long. Double the wire at the center and string five beads down to the end of the loop. Then twist the wire for a quarter of an inch to make a five-petal flower on a short stem.

String five more beads onto one of the wires and twist the wire back on itself to form a second flower and stem. Then string five beads on the other wire to make a third flower and stem. Continue by alternating the stems and flowers on the two sides of the main stem until you reach the end of the wire. Then add one or two other wires to make a main stem that holds about 15 flowers. The length of the stems and the number of flowers should vary a little to enliven the pattern of the corsage.

Make ten or twelve stems and then gather them together, add three or four green-glass leaves, and wrap the ends of the stems with green tape.

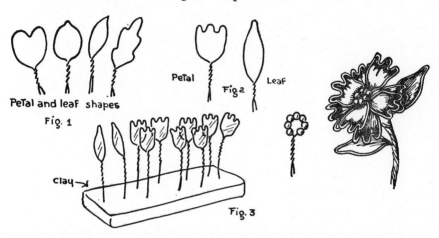

Petal and leaf shapes

Fig. 1

Petal   Fig 2   Leaf

clay→

Fig. 3

WIRE AND PLASTIC FLOWERS. Here is a relatively new way of making artificial flowers, which is enjoyed as a hobby by many people. The outlines of the flower petals are made of thin copper wire—about 20 gauge—and the frames are then dipped in liquid plastic and painted. The plastic, paints, wire, stem tape and other materials can be obtained at hobby shops and some ten-cent stores.

The flowers can be used for home and costume decorations, table and wall flowers, pins, corsages, hair and hair comb ornaments, earrings, buttons and buckles. In addition, you can twist the wire into many simple forms such as butterflies, leaves, fish, animals and human figures.

The flower pin shown in the drawings, which has eight petals and two leaves, is made as follows: cut ten 6-inch lengths of copper wire. Use one-half the length of each piece to make eight petals and two leaves shaped as in Fig. 2. Make the scallops on each petal with long-nosed pliers.

Dip each petal and leaf frame separately in the liquid plastic. Use a scooping motion to permit the plastic to form a skin across the open area in each frame. Withdraw the frames very slowly. Sometimes you may have to dip them into the plastic more than once to get the skin to form. If the skin breaks too often, it means that thinner (obtainable at hobby shops) should be added to the plastic. If air bubbles form in the skin, they can be removed by immediately dipping the frame in the plastic again.

After dipping each piece, insert the stem into a block of clay, which can be obtained at a hobby shop. The plastic will harden in about 10 minutes. The pieces can then be removed from the clay and set aside to harden for about three hours.

The pieces are then painted with a special plastic lacquer made for the purpose and obtainable at hobby shops. The colors are applied by brush on the backs of the petals and leaves, and show through the plastic. Colors and color combinations of all kinds are used. Bronze and black, for example, give a very striking effect. The leaves are painted green.

The flower is assembled as follows. Thread seven small seed beads on a 6-inch piece of thin wire. Make a small loop of the beads at one end of the wire for the center of the flower. Hold this center in the center of three of the petals and wrap the remaining wire around the petals to hold them together. Then add two or three petals at a time until all eight petals have been wired in place, bound to the first petals with the wire. Tie the leaves on the same way about an inch down the stem.

Fasten the flower to a pinback, using thin wire. Then wrap the stem with green stem or binding tape. Leave the pin open while wrapping the stem so that the wire used for fastening on the pinback will be covered.

Pins for boutonniéres are wired to stems with thin wire,

then covered with stem tape. Earring petals are wired together, one at a time, with thin wire. After an earring flower has been completed, the stems of the petals are cemented together at the base of the petals. When the cement has hardened, the stems are cut off close to the base and the flower is cemented to an earpiece.

TWISTED-WIRE FIGURES. With pliable wire you can make any number of human figures. They can also be used as place cards or party favors. Small figures can be wired to safety pins and used as lapel ornaments. The figures can be left unadorned or can be dressed with scraps of cloth to represent cowboys or other characters.

The drawings show three ways to make the figures. The first way is to bend a piece of wire to form the head, body and legs, and then twist on another piece of wire to form the arms.

For the second method, put two pieces of wire side by side and twist them around each other. The Y-shaped ends are the arms and legs. To make the head, twist a piece of wire twice around a pencil and then twist the ends under the arms.

Still another way to make the figures is to use two pieces of wire—one for the head, neck and arms, the other for the body, legs and feet. The lower piece is twisted around the upper one at the base of the neck. This is done before the lower piece is twisted to form the body.

Large figures which have heads about 1 inch high can be made with corks or wooden beads for heads. Faces cut from magazines can be glued to the corks. When completed, the little figures can be dressed in dozens of different ways. To make them stand up, glue their feet to squares of cardboard.

The cowboy may be dressed in a plaid shirt and a pair of yellow oilcloth pants laced together around the edges with thread or wool. The ten-gallon hat is made of yellow oilcloth.

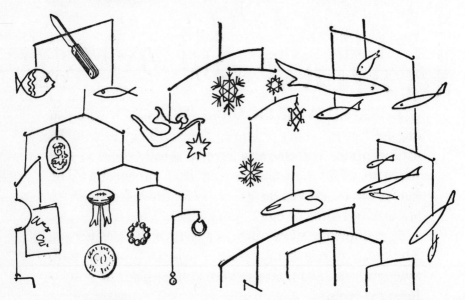

MOBILES. Mobiles are fun to make and fun to watch after they have been completed. The pieces that dangle from the wire framework of a mobile often look like shapes cut out from an abstract painting, but they may also represent actual objects, and can be made of any kind of material. Wire, cardboard, paper, plastic, thin sheet metal, wood, glass, Christmas-tree ornaments, dolls and other materials are all useful to the mobile artist.

Mobiles are created, as the name implies, to move. Basically, they consist of small forms suspended on fine wires, strings or threads, so they are free to move with the slightest air current, without touching one another.

You can invent your own mobiles or make some of those shown in the drawings. Your goal should be a pleasing and balanced composition that is simple and rhythmical, or has interesting geometrical design.

The wire rods of mobiles can be made of coat-hanger wire or other comparable wire. They always look well when painted black, but a variety of other colors and color combinations may be used. Mobiles are usually built from the bottom up, each little group of forms being brought into balance before it is connected to the next higher form or wire. Make sure that each little group is complete, including painting, before you balance them—testing out the balance on a knife blade, as shown. Even a thin coat of paint can throw a delicately adjusted mobile out of balance.

To balance cardboard or thin wooden forms, insert a pin where you think the balance point is. Let the form hang, and move the pin one way or the other until the form balances. Then drill a small hole through the pinhole, run thread through the hole, and tie. Continue from the lowest to the highest form or group of forms until you reach the main wire or string, balancing each group before securing it permanently.

You can find the balance point of forms made of metal and other materials through which you can't stick a pin by holding the form in a pair of tweezers.

Before starting to make a mobile, it is best to make a sketch of what you have in mind. Then you can work rather freely according to your plan, allowing variations that seem interesting to alter the original idea. The movement of a mobile adds to its complexity, so don't make them too cluttered. Eliminate and rearrange until your mobile has only what its needs for balance and design.

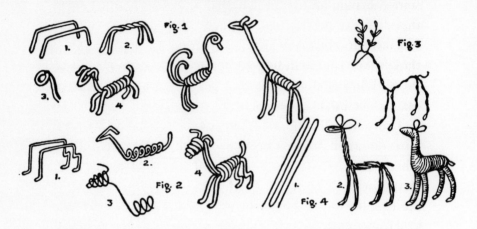

WIRE ANIMALS. There are several kinds of wire animals that are fun to make. You can try those shown here and then make up more of your own. Use pliable copper or iron wire, or wire solder. One of the animals is made of twisted wires. The other is made of a wire framework around which additional wire is wrapped to round out the body and head.

To make the dog, bend two pieces of wire 1 inch from each end to form four legs. Twist the center parts together to make the body. Then twist a piece of wire around a pencil to form the head and neck. Flatten the head to make a pointed nose. Attach the neck to the body by twisting its end around the front end of the body. Add the ears, made from a single piece of wire, and make the tail from another piece of wire twisted around the body at the top of the hind legs.

The giraffe and ostrich are made by the same method. If you want to pad out the body or head to get a particular shape or form, simply wrap more wire around it. Plastic wood, metallic cold solder and papier-mâché can also be used for this purpose.

To make the wrap-around deer, use a piece of wire 1½ feet long for a figure that will be about 1½ inches high. Fold the wire into four lengths, as shown. Then bend these four strands to form the general shape of the animal you want to make.

Make the ears first, by bending the two outside ends of the wire into loops. Make the head by bending the two strands outward. Then twist all four strands together to form the neck. Bend all four strands down and back up again for each front leg, so that each leg contains eight strands of wire. Leave a loop at the bottom of each leg for a hoof.

Shape the four strands for the body, and make the two hind legs in the same way as the forelegs. What is left of the wire will make the tail. The animal is then completed by wrapping wire around its body, legs, neck and head.

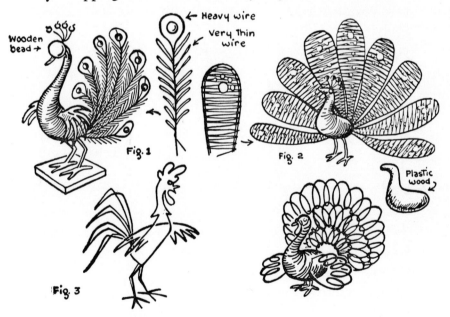

DECORATIVE BIRD FIGURES. The peacocks are two of my favorite wire figures. They are well worth the time and effort spent in putting them together. When completed, they can be made to stand up by stapling their feet to a small wooden base. The heads and bodies of the peacocks are made from fairly heavy copper wire bent to shape. They can be flat with fine wire wound around them, or else you can shape a rounded body from plastic wood, cold metallic solder or papier-mâché and then wrap wire around it. The eyes are beads which are cemented to short pieces of thin wire. The tail feathers are twisted to the body and further secured by cement.

The bright beads or buttons that decorate the tail of the peacock in Fig. 1 are strung on thin wire, then cemented in place before the tail feathers are fastened to the body. Sequins can also be used. In making the peacock shown in Fig. 2, each tail feather is completed by winding fine wire across it before the feathers are fastened in place. These feathers can be "brilliantized" by cementing small beads or sequins to them.

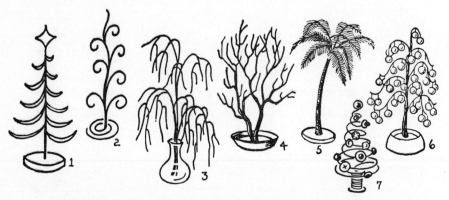

TREES FOR TABLE DECORATIONS. Soft iron wire and gleaming copper, steel, brass and aluminum wire can be used to make a number of conventional and stylized trees. They are made by cementing pieces of wire together.

Some of the more elaborate ones should be made slowly, since it takes time and patience to cut and fasten in place the many pieces of fine wire that make up the branches.

You can start by making the simple tree shown in Fig. 1. It can have a coiled-wire base or can be set in a wood or plastic base and it is crowned with a clear or colored plastic form. Another stylized tree is shown in Fig. 2. Or you can try your hand at making the graceful tree-form shown in Fig. 3. It can be mounted on a base or can be placed in a flower vase.

A more ambitious and very interesting project is to make a wire copy of a real tree with bare branches (Fig. 4). It can be mounted on a base or "planted" in a bowl filled with earth.

The palm tree shown in Fig. 5 is another interesting design, for which wire is particularly suitable. The trunk can be made from wires twisted together and covered with brown crêpe paper; or you can use a twig of real wood. The fine wires that make up the palm fronds are cemented in place. Each one is bent at an acute angle in the middle as shown.

Fig. 6 shows a wire and bead berry bush. Its berries can be of any and all colors or of a single color. Clear glass beads give a wonderful effect.

The spiral tree in Fig. 7 is easy to make and an attractive ornament. It can be mounted on a spool and can be decorated with beads, buttons or ten-cent-store sparklers.

FRUIT BASKET WALL DECORATION. Use 1/16-inch or heavier soft iron wire. The basket, which is really a half-basket, consists of an upper and lower semicircular frame. These are joined together by a number of pieces of wire—three or four vertical wires in the back to give rigidity, and ten or more slanting wires between the curved parts of the rings. The back wires should be hooked around the rings to give good strength. The front wires can be cemented, since there is no great strain on them. Several wires should be cemented across the bottom ring to provide a bottom for the basket.

WIRE PORTRAITS. Wire portraits are, in a way, like pencil drawings, but there is a knack to picking out the special, salient characteristics of each face and reproducing them with lines made of wire. Wire portraiture is closely akin to the art of the skilled cartoonist.

The drawings show examples of how excellent likenesses can be obtained by the use of wire. It is best to make a pencil sketch first and use it as a guide. Photographs can also, of course, be very helpful. Bend the wire pieces to the right shapes and cement them to cardboard or heavy paper, which can be framed when the portrait is finished.

SCROLLWORK BORDERS. Borders suggesting wrought iron are popular today and are easy to make. They are used chiefly on picture frames, mirrors, clocks and light-switch plates.

The drawings show several interesting designs, and you

will not find it difficult to devise others. Use thin soft iron, galvanized steel or copper wire, and bend each piece carefully to shape with pliers. Paint each piece dull black, if you want to be conventional; but brighter colors are lovely—white, red, blue, yellow, or whatever color goes with the room in which the piece is to be placed.

Switch-plate borders are usually black and the plate is also painted black. When the scrollwork pieces are completed, they are cemented in place. On wooden picture frames or mirror frames, the borders can be either cemented or stapled.

TABLE PICTURE EASELS. The large easel in Fig. 1 holds a picture. It is made from one piece of fairly stiff wire, the ends of which can be joined at the back, as shown, by cementing them inside a short piece of plastic or copper tubing. The little easel is fine for holding a snapshot or a small colored picture, such as the reproduction of some famous painting, which is 2 or 3 inches wide. You can find plenty of suitable pictures in magazines and can paste them to a cardboard back.

WIRE CONSTRUCTIONS. Wire constructions are abstract designs executed in different sizes and kinds of wire such as copper, brass, steel and stainless steel, to give varying textures. They are works of the imagination and their creation is a field in which you can experiment without limit.

Richard Lippold, head of the art department at Trenton Junior College in New Jersey, has specialized in this type

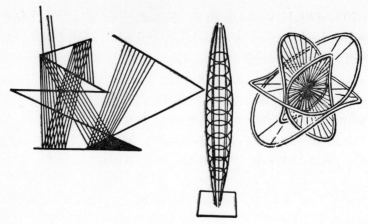

of work and his wire constructions are in many private and museum collections, including the Museum of Modern Art. Some are very large—several feet in height, while others can be balanced in the palm of the hand.

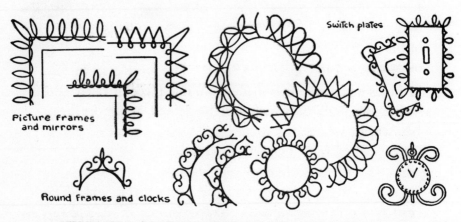

Switch plates

Picture frames and mirrors

Round frames and clocks

TWISTED-WIRE PICTURE FRAME. This ingeniously twisted picture frame is made of $\frac{1}{16}$-inch copper or aluminum wire. Bend it to the shape shown, using pliers and a rolling pin or some other cylindrical object as a jig or mandrel on which to form the circle. Join the ends with cellulose tape as shown.

Cut the snapshot or picture to be framed to form a circle as large as the outside diameter of the wire circle. Put it between a circle of cardboard and a circle of thin clear plastic, and fasten the three pieces together with small pieces of transparent tape. Then cement the picture to the back of the wire circle.

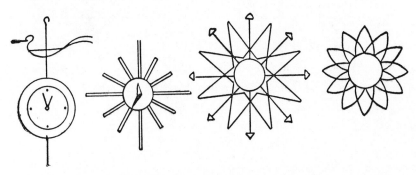

CLOCK AND MIRROR DECORATIONS. Dressing up clocks and mirrors with wire ornamentation is a popular pastime. The drawings show several patterns, of which only the starburst design, intended for a mirror, is difficult to make. The easiest way to do it is to make each of the eight-pointed pieces separately. Care must be taken, of course, to have all the pieces identical. This can be done by using a triangular jig of three nails driven into a board. The eight arrows can be made singly, or can consist of four long arrows with tips at each end. The pieces are cemented to the back of the mirror.

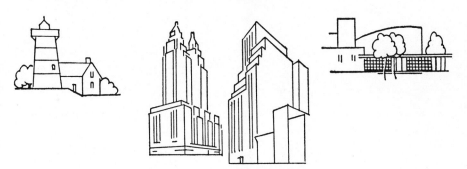

HOUSE AND BUILDING OUTLINE PICTURES. If you are architecturally minded—or even if you just own a home and like it—you may find it interesting to make a

reproduction of it and of skyscrapers and other buildings
as well, in wire. These reproductions are outlines made by
cementing pieces of thin wire to cardboard. Colors can be
added, such as green shutters, red chimneys, a green lawn,
and so on.

Wire models of this kind are interesting to make, and
the skyscraper outlines form fascinating compositions.
Thin, straight florists' wire is a good kind to use for a large
part of this work, which is a particularly suitable medium
for wire.